365

DAVID
LAWRENCE
PRESTON

ways to
be your own
life coach

howtobooks

Dedication

This book is dedicated to all those friends and colleagues from whom I have learned so much, and the many great teachers who have guided me on my journey (especially the greatest teacher of all – life itself).

Testimonials

On behalf of all the students on the Life Coaching course, I would like to place on record our sincere appreciation of David's skill and professionalism together with his teaching abilities. He is a fine example of your service.

(JAE – one of David Lawrence Preston's recent students)

I feel I have been very privileged to have been able to receive such professional, first class coaching. You were highly professional, have a wealth of expertise and knowledge and yet you still made me feel as though I had just found my best friend. I am so excited because I know you have given me the tools to start living life to the full. All you have taught me in these few weeks I will now pass on to my own children. What fantastic value. Oh and one last thing – you told me to think with my heart sometimes. That made me realise I have not done that for years – how liberating. Thank you from the bottom of my heart (and my head!).

JR, Poole

Thank you so much for your encouragement and advice. I can say hand on heart that you have been the single most inspirational person with regards to my confidence and personal development, which are very important to me. I cannot thank you enough for the help you have given me.

JH, Bournemouth

Published by How To Books Ltd,
3 Newtec Place, Magdalen Road,
Oxford, OX4 1RE, United Kingdom.
Tel: (01865) 793806. Fax: (01865) 248780.
email: info@howtobooks.co.uk
http://www.howtobooks.co.uk

First edition 2005
Reprinted 2006

British Library Cataloguing in Publication Data
A catalogue record for this book is available from
the British Library.

Produced for How To Books by Deer Park Productions, Tavistock
Typeset by *specialist* publishing services ltd, Milton Keynes/Montgomery
Printed and bound by Cromwell Press, Trowbridge, Wiltshire

Note: The material contained in this book is set out in good
faith for general guidance and no liability can be accepted
for loss or expense incurred as a result of relying in particular
circumstances on statements made in the book. The laws and
regulations are complex and liable to change, and readers should
check the current position with the relevant authorities before
making personal arrangements.

Contents

Welcome to *365 ways*
to be your own life coach

Since you're reading this, I imagine you want to make some changes to your life, but you're not entirely sure how to go about it. You're not alone. That's why there's been such a phenomenal growth in life coaching in Britain and many other countries in the past few years.

The first time I heard the term was in a talk by the inspirational motivational speaker and author, Anthony Robbins, ten years ago. 'Some people call me a guru,' he said, 'but that's not true. I'm not a guru, I'm a coach. I coach people to get the best out of themselves.'

Since then, life coaching has become big business. Training, diplomas and certificates are offered by a profusion of 'schools' and 'institutes' worldwide, although, unlike therapy and counselling, there are currently no formally recognised professional qualifications in the UK for life coaches. That's not to say these independent organisations are not very good, just unregulated.

Life coaches offer their services to individuals, groups and businesses, often at exorbitant rates. A friend of mine recently paid £375 for three, 55 minute, four-way telephone conversations with a life coach. That's over £9 for every minute of his share of attention from the coach! He claims to have benefited from the sessions, but obviously many of those who need help can't afford to pay that sort of money. Hopefully everyone can afford to invest in this book.

What do life coaches aim to do? Simply to support and encourage their clients in their personal and professional growth by helping them to identify and achieve their goals. They use a variety of conversational and written techniques to help them find the best way forward, strengthen their motivation and take action. Good coaches don't give advice, but help the client to find the answer for themselves.

It occurs to me that I have been a life coach for over 20 years, although I have only recently begun to refer to myself as such. I have unwittingly coached my children, friends, colleagues and students. I have also been a life coach to my clients (I have been a hypnotherapist for over ten years), and often found life coaching to be more useful to them than therapy.

Some of my 'coachees' completely turned their lives around and went on to great success in their chosen fields. None paid anything like £9 per minute, and neither need you. If you follow the tried and tested methods offered in this book, you can transform your life with no financial outlay other than the cover price.

I base my methods on three simple ideas. You will become very familiar with these in the weeks ahead:

- The TGROW method.
- Eight Steps to Success.
- The ITIA formula.

I believe the best coach for you is you, and I aim to give free rein to him or her. This book will show you exactly what you need to do to turn yourself into your own life coach. There are 365 priceless ideas, exercises and skills to learn from and apply.

I want you to get more from this book than a warm feeling. I want you to put these principles and techniques into practice so you will reap the rewards. But you won't gain full benefit if you merely read my words. That would be like expecting to get better by gazing at the label on the bottle without actually taking the medicine.

I guarantee: if you read the material carefully and use what you learn, big changes will take place. A year from now you'll look back with amazement on all you've achieved.

So let's get started.

David Lawrence Preston
david@davidlawrencepreston.co.uk
www.davidlawrencepreston.co.uk

1 How To Be Your Own Life Coach – An Overview

The TGROW method

The TGROW method is widely used in life coaching sessions. In each session life coaches take their clients through five steps, although not necessarily in sequence.

The letters stand for:

Theme
Goals
Reality
Options
Will

Theme

What's on your mind right now? Where do your priorities lie? Are there any problems in any particular area of your life which you feel need attention? Which features of your life are you most keen to change?

- **Health**: do you have sufficient energy to carry you through each day, and, if not, what are you going to do about it?

- **Career**: are there any issues in your working life or business activities which need attending to?

- **Money**: have you any financial problems that need dealing with?

- **Home life**: is everything OK with the people you live with, your husband/wife/partner, your children and wider family?

- **Social relationships**: are you getting pleasure from an active, varied and fulfilling social life?

- ■   **Hobbies**: do you have interests and pastimes that provide enjoyment and take your mind off the pressures of life?

- ■   **Lifestyle**: how do you want to live? What do you want to experience? Do you have the way of life you would ideally choose for yourself? If not, are you clear what would be the perfect lifestyle for you, and what you would like to change?

- ■   **Personal development and spiritual life**: does your self-esteem need a boost, or are you considering becoming involved with a particular religious group, or taking up a spiritual practice such as prayer or meditation?

- ■   What, if anything, do you no longer want in your life?

In reality, of course, you can't separate out these areas of your life, because they have a significant effect on each other. Your work affects your family life, stress levels, intimate relationships and health, and soaks up energy you may prefer to devote to your hobbies and pastimes. Equally, your home and family life impinges on your effectiveness at work, and so on.

Goals

Are you clear on your goals? Indeed, do you have any goals – long, medium or short-term? If you did have any goals, what would they be, and can you think of anything you can start doing now that would move you closer towards them?

Is there one goal which, if achieved, could make the others fall into place and transform your life? Would, for instance, a career or business goal solve a pressing financial problem and allow you to pursue a cherished hobby or fulfil a longing to travel? If so, is there something you could do within the next two weeks, seven days, or even today to make a start?

We'll take a more detailed look at the goal setting process in the pages ahead, and suggest a useful goal setting pro-forma.

Reality

While it is important to have goals, it's also important to be realistic about your chances of achieving them. Setting yourself challenging goals within impractical deadlines can be very damaging, because you are almost certain to fail. Make sure you're not asking the impossible of yourself.

Take stock of your present situation. Try to understand all the factors which impact on your goals:

- Where are you now in relation to each goal?

- What resources do you have? What do you need? How will you acquire them?

- Do you have all the knowledge, skills and personal qualities you require?

- What's been holding you back? Are there any obstacles? How significant are they?

- What have you done so far? Did it work? What stopped you going further?

Options

How many options do you have for achieving your goals? List them. Do some research: read widely, surf the net, ask around. Rule nothing out at this stage, no matter how far fetched it seems.

Where there are several feasible options available, look at each in turn. Identify those that seem best and consider how they will achieve your desired outcome. Look back over your options from time to time; reviewing them may spark off new ideas.

Will

Decide on the actions you will take and commit yourself to them. When you work through TGROW systematically, your decisions are based on a clear grasp of the issues. Set tasks, deadlines and timescales, and write them down. As you proceed, monitor the results to make sure your actions are taking you closer to your goals. If not, do something different, that's more likely to take you there.

Simple enough, isn't it? If it seems daunting, don't worry: we'll be clarifying each of these steps in the following pages and offering a plethora of ideas to make them practical, realistic, effective and exciting.

Let's work through the process to gain a better understanding of how it operates. (You can photocopy any of the next few pages and use them as a template if you wish.)

1

Choose one of your goals. (If you can't think of any, *imagine* something you would like to achieve.) Spend some time on the next few pages.

Description of your goal (in present tense):

....

....

Life area: (e.g. work, family, hobbies, health, etc):

....

Target date

....

Benefits when achieved:

....

....

Intermediate steps (with dates):

....

....

Support/infrastructure required:

....

....

How will you know when you've achieved it?

....

....

I confirm that this is a true description of my goal, and that I am committed to achieving it.

Your signature .... Today's date ....

Date for review ....

2 Where are you now in relation to this goal?

What actions have you taken so far?

....

....

What worked? What didn't?

....

....

What stopped you going further? Are there any obstacles, major or minor, and what are they?

....

....

How much control do you have over them?

....

....

What resources do you have?

....

....

What do you need, and how will you acquire them?

....

....

What new knowledge, skills and personal qualities do you need?

....

....

What else is on your mind concerning this goal?

....

....

3 What options do you have for reaching your goal?

List all the alternatives – rule nothing out at this stage	Column (b) Leave blank for now	Column (c) Leave blank for now
1		
2		
3		
4		
5		
6		
7		
8		

If you can think of more than eight – great! Use a separate sheet.

4

Once you have finished your list of options, go through each of them in detail. Examine them carefully, and tick those that seem most likely to achieve the outcome you want in column (b). Alternatively, rank them from 1 to 8, 1 being the most likely and 8 the least likely.

What is your level of commitment to pursuing each option? Write a number between zero and ten in column (c) next to each tick, where ten means totally and irrevocably committed, and zero means no commitment at all. (If you choose zero, ask yourself why did I tick it?)

5

Write an action plan. Establish your priorities, set deadlines, and commit to them. Jot down anything else that will help.

Action	By (date)	Notes
1		
2		
3		
4		
5		
6		

If six isn't enough, that's fine, use a separate sheet.

Congratulations – you've just worked through the TGROW method for the first time. You now have some working documents which you can refer to and refine whenever you review your goals and plans, which you should do regularly.

So that's a broad overview of the process. Now – let's step back and examine it in more detail.

What is life coaching?

The essence of life coaching is very simple. It is a guided discussion, or series of discussions, between two people (sometimes more – life coaching can take place in groups), either face to face, on the telephone or via other electronic means. Its purpose is to guide the client to more success, happiness and wellbeing than they are currently experiencing.

The coach supports the client to learn new ways of working, improve their performance and get better results. Sometimes clients have a vague feeling that life could be better or something's wrong, but can't put their finger on it. Often they know what they want, but don't know how to get it. Coaches help them to decide.

Some coaches have themselves achieved at a high level. Eileen Mulligan, for example, author of *Life Coaching*, built up a £million company in the beauty industry and won awards for enterprise before becoming a successful business consultant and personal coach. Julia McCutcheon, coach to many well known authors, had an impressive track record in the publishing world, and many management coaches can claim substantial achievements in industry and commerce.

However, this is not absolutely necessary. Many outstanding life coaches have little or no experience in the subject areas in which they coach their clients. In similar vein, Sir Alex Ferguson and Arsene Wenger, coaches to Britain's most illustrious soccer teams, Manchester United and Arsenal, were not particularly successful as players, but this has not prevented them from guiding their teams to many trophies. Most film directors were not noted as actors, and most of the singing teachers who coach entertainment megastars were never famous themselves, but they don't have to be; they know how to bring the best out of their charges, and that's what matters.

Because the term 'life coaching' is relatively new, it's important to understand exactly what it is and what it is not.

Life coaching *is*:

- Concerned with choosing where you want to be and how to get there. It focuses on the **here and now** and the *future*.

- Based on the premise that the future doesn't have to equate to the past, the past is relevant only if it is likely to seriously affect the results of the coaching.

- A process which helps you think about your current circumstances and clarify your goals in a balanced way in every area of your life.

- About exploring your thoughts, feelings and experiences to promote learning and constructive action. You can learn to improve your communication skills, be more confident, motivated and proactive, handle stress, cultivate self-discipline, create positive attitudes and change unproductive behaviours.

- A catalyst. Insights and learning are as likely to emerge *between* coaching sessions as much as *during* them.

- A useful tool for putting together a plan to realise your aspirations in life.

Life coaching is *not*:

- Counselling or therapy. It does not seek to resolve psychological and emotional issues (although this can happen). Reputable life coaches who perceive a need for therapy in a client would recommend consulting a therapist even if they were trained therapists themselves (which some are). They know that confusing therapy with coaching is unhelpful.

- Life coaches imposing their views on the client or solving their problems for them. They do not take responsibility away from their clients. They help them find their own way, even if it is not the way the coach would have suggested.

- A short-term measure just to cope with current issues. It takes a long-term view, although it is also concerned with today's actions.

I recently coached an 18-year-old girl. Her father had taken her out of school just before she was due to take her GCSE examinations and relocated to a foreign country where she could not speak the language. On her return to England, she was hampered by her lack of qualifications and work experience and racked with self-doubt. I gently discouraged her from dwelling on the past. I paid no attention to her self-pity, and turned her attention to what she wanted and what she needed to do to make it possible.

We formulated an action plan which involved returning to college part-time to get qualified while working in the evenings and at weekends to support herself. Despite her past misfortunes, she's now well on the way to getting the job in the travel industry that she longs for.

Self-coaching

Self-coaching is being a coach to yourself. Just as life coaches have a duty of care to their clients, as self-coach you must acknowledge your duty of care to yourself. This includes fostering your own wellbeing, being willing to recognise your weaknesses as well as your strengths, enjoying your successes and being honest enough to admit when things aren't going to plan.

Just as life coaches talk things through with their clients and make notes, self-coaches talk things through with themselves, ask constructive questions and then write down the main points in the form of a plan for future reference. As you will see, effective self-coaching boils down to asking the *right* questions of themselves, other people, published and electronic sources, and then acting on the answers that come from external sources and within.

Life coaches and their clients make time to speak regularly, usually weekly. Similarly, as a self-coach, you must be willing to put aside time for yourself, to read, learn and apply the tools and techniques.

6

Buy a notebook to use as your Self-Coaching Journal. Alternatively, an A4 size ringbinder would be just as good. Use it to record your goals, plans, actions taken and their results. Write down your thoughts on your progress. Include ideas for self-development, inspirational anecdotes, quotations, memory joggers and so on. Note what's going right, what's not working, what's holding you back, and what you intend to do about it. Use it like a scrap book, pasting journal articles and press cuttings, etc.

Date every entry – then you can trace your development and progress over the months and years ahead. Update it daily if possible; if not, at least once a week.

7

What kind of person would you expect a life coach to be? What qualities, attitudes and skills would he or she possess? Jot down your thoughts in your Self-Coaching Journal.

Before looking at the questions opposite, consider which of these qualities you need to develop in yourself as a self-coach.

Some qualities of a good life coach	Which did you think of?	Which do you need to develop in yourself?
Excellent listening and communication skills.		
Neither judgmental nor critical of others.		
Respect client confidentiality.		
Patient and flexible, open, honest and friendly.		
Make their clients feel valued and understood.		
Able to enthuse and motivate others, and raise their spirits.		
Insight to perceive and suggest options for the client.		
Believe in their clients 100 per cent.		
Take clients seriously and be totally committed to their success and wellbeing.		
Have a positive attitude to setbacks.		
Know how to hold their clients to account if they fail to live up to their promises or meet their deadlines (without destroying their self-confidence).		
Know how to support their clients to achieve more than they otherwise would.		

8

Here are some of the qualities and skills of a good self-coach. Which do you already have? Which do you need to work on?

Do you/are you:	Yes/no?	Need to work on?
Willing to listen to your inner self?		
A positive thinker?		
Neither judgmental nor critical of yourself?		
Value and understand yourself?		
Believe in yourself and take yourself and your desires seriously?		
Committed to creating your own success and wellbeing?		
Understand that, in self-coaching, there is no such thing as failure, only feedback?		
Able to hold yourself to account if you fail to meet your obligations?		
Know how to support yourself to achieve more than you have so far? (Probably not; why else would you be reading this?)		

Don't worry if you can't honestly answer 'yes' to all of these questions just yet. Keep applying the 365 principles and practices, and before long you will!

9   Are you ready to self-coach?

	Yes	No
Do you have your Self-Coaching Journal and are you clear on how you are going to use it?		
Are you willing to set aside time in advance each day to read, do the exercises and carry out the assignments?		
Are you ready to make changes, acquire new skills and eliminate negative habit patterns?		
Do you agree to keep going, even when it seems easier to give up?		
Are you ready to choose a more enthusiastic and optimistic attitude from now on?		

Hopefully you have answered 'yes' to all of these. So let's continue.

Why self-coaching works: Cause and Effect

" *Don't judge each day by the harvest you reap, but by the seeds you sow.*

Eastern proverb "

Cause and Effect is one of the fundamental principles underlying the workings of the universe. It applies in the natural sciences (physics, chemistry, astronomy, etc) and social sciences (psychology, sociology, economics, etc), and explains not only why life on Earth is as it is, but also why *your* life is as it is.

The principle states that everything that exists is the result of a cause, some action. Moreover, every human action is preceded by a thought, either conscious or subconscious. Obviously not every thought leads to an action, but equally there can be no action without a preceding thought.

In other words, what you sow you reap, and what you reap, you sow. You get out of life what you put into it, and when you change the causes that shape your life – primarily your thoughts, words and actions – you get different results.

Since your thoughts, words and actions are under your control (you may not yet think so, but they are), evidently you control the circumstances of your life. That's why many individuals brought up in abject poverty, or orphaned, physically handicapped, or emotionally or sexually abused, have been able to put their early disadvantages behind them and enjoy happy and fulfilling lives.

You make the Principle of Cause and Effect work for you by sowing new, improved seeds. As you grow in self-awareness and apply the TGROW method, the Eight Steps (see page 21) and ITIA formula (see page 52), you reap a new, more fulfilling and more abundant harvest.

Obviously not everyone who has turned their life around has *consciously* applied these techniques, but they have gone through the same progression nevertheless. Here's an example:

'Have big dreams, son.'

Who do you think this story is about?

As a boy growing up on one of the toughest estates in Northern England, this young man faced brutality every day of his life. His response was to meet violence with violence. By the age of ten, he was known as the toughest kid on the block. No one around him believed that things could be any different; hardly anyone he knew had made very much of their lives. But he had one big advantage over his contemporaries – his Mum. 'Have big dreams, son,' she would say, 'because there's nothing you can't achieve.'

He did have a dream – he loved reading and wanted to be an English teacher, but that ambition all but died when he was rejected by the local grammar school and sent to a rough secondary school. (He discovered years later that he had actually passed the entrance exam, but was excluded because his reputation had preceded him.) He was finally expelled at 15 for vandalism.

Several years of heavy drinking and tedious factory jobs followed, then a spell in prison for beating someone up at a football match. This turned out to be the turning point: during his incarceration he realised that his behaviour was getting him nowhere, and resolved to change. Something inside told him that no matter what had gone before, he could make a new start. So he set himself some goals.

When he came out he started a business buying up run-down houses, doing them up and selling them. Then one day he spotted a newspaper advertisement for actors to take part in a new television drama about a group of unemployed construction workers seeking work in Germany. Impressed by his hard exterior and blunt manner, they offered him the part of Oz, the truculent bricklayer, his first step on the road to fame and fortune. He has since gone on to become an internationally acclaimed entertainer, continually in demand.

Did you recognise this as the story of Jimmy Nail, TV actor, film star, scriptwriter, director, singer, songwriter and musician?

11

Let's consider Jimmy Nail's example in more detail. How do you account for his transformation? What were the 'causes' that produced the success, happiness and prosperity that must have been beyond his wildest dreams in his teens and early twenties? Jot down a few notes (before you look at the list below).

Jimmy Nail brought into play the Law of Cause and Effect. He may not have been consciously aware that his thoughts and imagination were prime causes, but even so, his personal transformation started with a change that took place *between his ears*.

1   He created an intention and set himself some goals.

2   He used the power of his mind to change bad habits, build positive beliefs and visualise a successful future.

3   He acquired new knowledge, learned new skills (first as a builder and businessman, then as an actor/writer/musician, etc) and progressively turned himself into the person he needed to be to realise his ambitions.

4   He candidly evaluated his situation.

5   He considered his options and made a plan.

6   He took action – lots of it.

7   He kept track of the results of his actions and adjusted his strategy. Moreover, when a new opportunity presented itself, he grabbed it with both hands.

8   He kept going, showing patience and persistence, both in setting up his business, then establishing himself as an entertainer.

These are the eight fundamental steps of self-coaching. The ITIA formula and TGROW method are embedded in them.

Jimmy Nail has made an outstanding success of his life. He has demonstrated one of the elementary truths basic to self-coaching – the future does not equal the past. Carry on laying the same 'causes', and we get the same results; change the 'causes' and the 'effects' change too.

Jimmy Nail could have continued with his devil-may-care tough-guy behaviour, but once he realised that more of the same would only bring more of the same, he set out on a new course.

Like Jimmy Nail, you have a past. You could carry on laying down the same 'causes', or you could set new goals, change how you think, change what you imagine about the future, and change how you conduct yourself. In other words, you can make the Principle of Cause and Effect work for you. That's what self-coaching is all about.

Eight steps to success

1   Set clear goals.

2   Use the power of your mind – think positively, undo negative conditioning, build positive beliefs and use your imagination to help you create the life you want.

3   Acquire the knowledge, qualities and new skills you need; become the person you need to be to realise your ambitions.

4   Evaluate your current situation.

5   Consider your options.

6   Take action – the right action, and lots of it.

7   Monitor your progress and make adjustments if necessary.

8   Keep going. Plug into the power of persistence.

12

Self-coaching is all about guiding yourself to happiness and success. What do these terms mean to you? Write your personal definitions of 'happiness' and 'success'.

To me, happiness means

....

....

To me, success means

....

....

13

In your Self-Coaching Journal list what 'success' means to you regarding your:

■ Health and fitness.

■ Career, work and business activities.

■ Financial affairs.

■ Home life and family relationships.

■ Social relationships and friendships.

■ Hobbies and pastimes.

■ Lifestyle.

■ Personal development and spiritual life.

How would you *know* if you were successful in each of these life areas?

14

What do you think has held you back in life so far? Write down six things that have stopped you being as successful as you would like in the grid below.

1	
2	
3	
4	
5	
6	

15

List three ways in which you hope this book will help you be more successful.

1	
2	
3	

2 Step one: clear intentions – choosing your goals

> *Anyone who consciously becomes a goal setter, writes them down, and frequently thinks and talks about them will notice an immediate and dramatic improvement in their level of accomplishment, even if they've done very little with their lives before.*
>
> **Brian Tracy**

Why goals matter

Goals are simply your intentions specified, clarified and written down, with deadlines.

From an early age your accomplishments and your happiness are determined by your intentions, the decisions you make and the extent to which you carry them through.

In the Western world we are faced with an overwhelming number of choices. A modern superstore has over 100,000 lines – compare this to the range available to our grandparents just a few decades ago, or to people in many other parts of the world. Imagine entering a superstore with no idea of what you wanted to buy and no idea of how much you could afford to spend. You'd be in total confusion.

Until you narrow down your choices in a meaningful way, you're like a scattergun, firing shots in all directions, hoping to hit something, but not sure what that may be. Once you decide which choices are most likely to bring you happiness and fulfilment, decisions become very much easier. Gone is the hesitancy, self-doubt and stress. You're clear on what you want, and ready to go out and get it.

Life coaches help their clients to be clear about what they want. Setting personal goals also lies at the heart of self-coaching. If you're not clear where you want to get to, how can you map out your journey? How do you know if you're heading in the right direction? How do you know when you've arrived?

You need goals on several different levels:

- Major (long-term) goals, which define the overall direction and shape of your life.

- Medium-term goals, the stepping stones that bring the long-term goals into focus.

- Short-term goals, which contribute to your medium-term goals and provide a framework for your day to day actions.

16

One of the main reasons why some people don't achieve very much or enjoy life to the full is that they're not clear what they want. This is illustrated perfectly by Lewis Carroll in a scene from *Alice in Wonderland*. Alice, wandering lost in the woods, encounters the Cheshire Cat sitting on a branch, grinning.

'Cheshire Puss,' Alice began rather timidly, 'would you tell me please, which way I ought to go from here?'
'That depends a good deal on where you want to get to,' said the cat.
'I don't much care where...' said Alice.
'Then it doesn't matter which way you go,' said the cat.
'... so long as I get somewhere,' Alice added by way of explanation.
'Oh you're sure to do that,' said the cat, 'if you only walk long enough.'

What point do you think Lewis Carroll was making when he wrote this scene?

Everyone has goals. For some it is to find the next meal, for others to get through the day. Others set more ambitious goals, like completing an important piece of work or completing a marathon. You set goals all the time, whether you realise it or not. When you wake up, you mentally set yourself the goal of getting washed and dressed and arriving at work on time. Each of these goals comprises many sub-goals, such as having breakfast, starting the car or arriving at the bus stop in time for the bus, and putting your shoes on the correct feet. Sometimes these goals are imposed on you by other people, such as the children, your partner or boss.

Without thinking too hard write down your immediate goals – those that are preoccupying you right now.

....

....

Examine your list. How do you feel about what you've written?

Your values

The road to happiness lies in two simple principles: find what it is that interests you and you can do well, and when you find it, put your whole soul into it – every bit of energy and ambition and natural ability you have.

John D. Rockefeller

Goal setting is a vital skill. But before you establish your goals, you must step back and decide what is really important to you in life. These are your values. It's important that your goals reflect your ideals and interests and make full use of your talents.

For your goals to be truly motivating and valuable, they must be:

- Grounded in your deepest values. You must have a clear idea of what's important to you and the kind of person you want to be.

- Balanced. A balanced life is one where each life area is in harmony.

- Consistent and complementary. It's pointless setting goals that contradict each other.

- Physically possible (for you).

Let's consider your values.

18

Your values are ideas, personal qualities and moral codes to which you are drawn. Only when you express your true values are you being true to yourself, and only then can you feel comfortable in your own skin.

Use the exercises on the next few pages to think long and hard about your values and prioritise them. Start by taking a pen and paper and consider: what do you most want out of life? Write your thoughts in your Self-Coaching Journal.

19

List the six things you most want to happen in the world. What for you would make the world a better place?

How strongly do you feel about them? Write a number between zero and ten in the right hand column, where ten means you feel it strongly in every cell of your body, and zero no strength of feeling at all.

Six things I want to happen in the world.	How strongly I feel about it.
1	
2	
3	
4	
5	
6	

20

Take a good look at yourself.

■ What do you most look forward to?

■ What really gets you excited?

■ Look at your bookshelves, your CD and video/DVD collection, the pictures on your wall. What do they say about you?

■ What TV and radio programmes do you enjoy? Conversely, what do you dislike?

■ What turns you off or fills you with disgust?

21

What activities give or have given you the greatest feeling of *achievement*? In which areas of your life have you achieved the most personal fulfilment?

22

The secret of creating a happy life is to do more of what you enjoy: from that comes happiness, enthusiasm, motivation and energy. So what activities do you *enjoy* the most? Also, what *don't* you enjoy? What would you like to clear out (physically and mentally) to make room for something better?

23

What do you stand for? What, if anything, would you defend with your life if necessary? What does this say about you?

24

If your life was perfect in every respect and you were too, what would it *look* like? *Feel* like? *Sound* like? *Be* like?

25

Supposing you had only six months to live, what would you do with your remaining time?

26

Think back to important incidents in your life where you felt compelled to act or speak out, regardless of the consequences, or where you didn't and wish you had. What do they have in common? Is there a pattern? If so, what is it?

27

Listen to your inner self. Spend a few minutes each day relaxing in a comfortable chair, close your eyes, slow your breathing and let your muscles relax (there's more about this on page 93, and in the companion book, *365 Steps to Self-Confidence*). Ask your inner self, 'What is important to me?' 'What do I most value in a job, relationship, hobby, myself, my friends, etc?' Allow yourself to daydream. When you open your eyes, write down anything that comes to mind.

28

Now look at everything you've written from section 18 to 27 and list your top ten values. Examples could include achievement, compassion, environment, health, honesty, generosity, family, love, enterprise, fun, fairness, security, independence, spirituality, etc.

Rank them, and say what you mean by each of them on the grid below. If ten isn't enough, use a separate sheet.

Your top values	What each value means to you
1	
2	
3	
4	
5	
6	
7	
8	
9	
10	

Benefits of setting goals

Success in life could be defined as the continued expansion of happiness and the progressive realisation of worthy goals.

Dr Deepak Chopra

29 Research shows conclusively that people who consciously set themselves goals accomplish far more than their contemporaries.

In a very famous study at Harvard University in 1953, only three per cent of the graduating class was found to have written goals and a plan for achieving them. Twenty years later, these three per cent had accomplished more and accumulated more in financial terms than the other ninety-seven per cent combined! Moreover, they were happier and more fulfilled.

Subsequent studies confirmed these results. Why do you think this is?

30 Why are goals so important? Your goals are present-day mental images of future events. They keep your mind firmly focused on what you want. Successful people, when not actively doing something about their goals, are *thinking* about them, *visualising* them, *imagining* and *feeling* them already accomplished.

This makes a major impact on your subconscious mind. The subconscious houses, among other things, a sophisticated automatic guidance system, like an autopilot. Its job is to seek out whatever you consistently focus your attention upon. Setting goals specifies the 'co-ordinates'. The autopilot then guides you towards your specified target by, for example, alerting you to opportunities and providing the impulse to take action.

If you fail to set clear goals, that is, select a destination, the autopilot is confused. It doesn't know where exactly you want to go, so it takes you round and round in circles like a missile that has been fired without programming in a target. Eventually, like the missile, you run out of energy, give up, or self-destruct.

It's been said that human beings are like bicycles – as long as we steer and keep pedalling we stay upright, but when we let go of the handlebars or stop pedalling we lose momentum, wobble and fall off.

The subconscious doesn't reason or ask questions, it simply does as it's told. If you let it know, explicitly or implicitly, that you have no direction in mind, fine! As the Cheshire Cat pointed out to Alice, any direction will do.

Do you give your subconscious autopilot clear coordinates?

31

Another advantage of clear goals is that they turn *frenetic* action into *effective* action. Many people are busy, but busy-ness is only the same as effectiveness if actions are goal-directed. A marathon runner heading off in the wrong direction could cover the same distance and burn up as much energy as the other competitors, but wouldn't win the race. Would you go to a booking office and ask for a ticket without saying where you want to go? Of course not!

Do you know where you want to go? Is your destination clear? Have you booked your trip?

32

When you're clear on your goals, you often find you attract people who can support and help you. People who themselves have a sense of purpose in their lives are drawn to you, and you to them, and the people you mix with have an enormous effect on you.

Do you attract positive, go-ahead people who help and encourage you to make the most of life?

33

Appropriate, meaningful goals provide powerful motivation, especially when you are clear why you want to accomplish them. A realistic, attainable, challenging and desirable goal creates energy and enthusiasm, and the new skills and personal qualities you develop tap into the vast reserves of creativity, intuition and imagination that lie within you. Your confidence grows, and you begin to feel (perhaps for the first time) that you're in charge of your own future.

Do you feel that you are in charge of your own future? Does this future inspire, energise and motivate you?

34

An enthusiastic teenager made a list of all the things he wanted to achieve. When he had finished, he had written down 117. Many were typical of a 15 year-old, but his ambitions also extended to climbing Mount Everest, visiting every country in the world and even flying to the moon.

By the time that young man was 47 years old he had ticked off 103 of his goals, including flying to the moon. His name was John Goddard, one of the Apollo astronauts. He is a perfect example of what can be accomplished by a person with challenging, clear-cut goals.

When you were a teenager, what were your major goals? How many of them have you achieved?

Your mission

> Here is a test to find whether your mission on earth is finished.
> If you're alive, it isn't.
>
> **Richard Bach**

35

There's nothing more important than finding a sense of purpose that gives your life meaning, and inspires and motivates you.

Arianna Huffington makes the point succinctly in her book, *The Fourth Instinct*:

'Give a gibbon a mate, a peaceful stretch of jungle and plenty of figs to munch on, and he will most likely live in contentment for the rest of his days. Give a man or woman an environment correspondingly idyllic – say, a successful career, adorable children and all the comforts civilization has to offer – and we feel dissatisfied, restless and vaguely aware that there is something very important missing from our lives.'

As a human being, your life is about much more than munching on figs. You need purpose; you need direction.

36

In your Self-Coaching Journal write a short paragraph that summarises your feelings about your life's purpose. This is your **mission statement**. It expresses what you would like your life to be about and how you can find fulfilment in a way which benefits others as well as yourself.

A typical mission statement could be:

■ My mission is to play my part in conserving the environment.

■ I am an entertainer. My role in life is to bring people happiness.

■ My mission is to help combat discrimination wherever I find it.

■ My role is to work for young people and fight cruelty to children.

- I love gardening. My mission is to make the world a more beautiful place.

- My mission is to make lots of money so I can plough it into good causes.

- My role is to design and make beautiful clothes that help people feel good about themselves.

- My mission is to spread love, peace and happiness to everyone I meet.

37

What would you like to see written about yourself in the obituary columns when you die, or alternatively, what you would like your children and grandchildren to tell *their* children about you?

Record it in your Self-Coaching Journal.

38

Imagine you are 90 years old, reflecting on your life. What are you most proud of? Have you accomplished everything you wanted so far? If not, what have you *not* done? On what have you missed out? What would you like to do with your remaining time?

Jot down your thoughts.

39

Finding your purpose is not an intellectual process – you must get in touch with your inner self. Tonight and for the next few days, ask your intuition to work on your mission statement just before you drop off to sleep.

In the morning write down anything relevant that comes into your mind, or draw a picture, chart or diagram.

40

Spend time in nature. The peace and tranquillity will quieten your mental chatter and allow you to focus on what's really important to you. Take a small notebook with you and write down anything that seems relevant, or, if you prefer, use a voice recorder.

41

Ask yourself (and write down the answers):

- If I could achieve anything I wanted with no possibility of failure, what would it be?

- If I won ten million pounds, euros or dollars (or any other currency) in a lottery and I wanted to use them to benefit humankind, how would I spend them?

- If I could have three wishes granted, what would they be?

- If I inherited a fortune, what would I do for a career even if I were not paid to do it?

42

What did you enjoy as a child (children are more closely in touch with their intuition)? If you can't remember, go through old photo albums or scrapbooks, or ask your parents, brothers and sisters for their recollections.

Ask yourself how you build on these things, do more of them or do them more often. Write down your answers.

43

Reflect on the coincidences in your life. Do the same people, events, problems or opportunities keep cropping up? Is there a pattern? Is it possible that your subconscious autopilot has been trying to guide you?

44

Having completed the above exercises, reflect on what they reveal about your inner desires and inclinations. Then write your mission statement and record it in your Self-Coaching Journal.

Check: does it state how you intend to benefit others as well as yourself?

Setting your goals

" *I believe you came into the world to accomplish something, and that the something you came to accomplish is not small or insignificant. That's not worthy of you. You came here to make a major contribution to life on this planet.*

Paul Solomon "

45

Find the right vehicle

Setting *major* goals is about finding the right vehicle for pursuing your mission and bringing your dreams into reality. *Minor* goals should lead to major goals and provide variety and light relief.

Naturally, individuals with similar missions may pursue them in different ways. One who wishes to help homeless young people, for instance, could train as a social worker and find employment with a local authority; another may volunteer to work in a charity shop or raise money in other ways. Another may work in an information and advice centre, or campaign through a political organisation, or help organise a hostel or soup run. All would say they had the same aim, but express it in different ways.

Similarly, not everyone would feel comfortable running their own business, while others thrive working for themselves. Many do not enjoy working for large organisations, but others make their greatest contribution this way. Some like to lead; others follow. Some prefer to go it alone; others are more comfortable working as part of a team.

Think carefully about your long term aspirations and ask yourself: 'What is the right vehicle for me?'

46

The next few pages offer clear guidelines for establishing your goals. Use the goal setting pro-forma (1, on pages 6–7), together with the guidelines on the next few pages. Photocopy sufficient for your needs; you'll need one copy for each goal. If you are using a ringbinder for your Self-Coaching Journal you can file them there.

47

State each goal in positive terms – goals are supposed to be what you want from life, not what you don't want. Use simple, straightforward language such as 'My goal is to…' or 'I want…' or 'I have'.
Under 'life area', choose from:

1   Health.

2   Career.

3   Money.

4   Home/family life.

5   Social life.

6   Hobbies and pastimes.

7   Lifestyle.

8   Personal development/spiritual life.

If you don't like my classifications, by all means choose your own.
Don't worry if you can't think of something in every area. Not every life area is of equal importance at any one time, and your priorities will change; 12 months from now a life area that doesn't seem that important now will probably assume greater importance, and vice versa.

48

State your goals in the present tense. Express than as if already happening, not as future events. For example, 'I am the proud winner of an Olympic medal,' *not*, 'I will aim to win an Olympic medal.'

49

Establish the date by which you intend to accomplish each goal. A programme of goals is not a wish list, but a statement of your intentions. Without deadlines they have little motivational power and no urgency.

Make your target dates challenging but realistic; setting ambitious goals within impossible deadlines can be demotivating and damaging. Instead, choose realistic deadlines and work steadily towards them.

Some goals lend themselves to a firm deadline, such as becoming a vegetarian, setting up a business, visiting Moscow, buying a car, decorating the living room, etc. Others (including many personal development goals) don't suddenly come to fruition on a particular day. Building confidence and self-belief, for instance, is an ongoing process. With these goals, write 'ongoing' (as long as this is not a cop-out and you do intend to work on them).

50

On your goals pro-formas write down all the benefits that will accrue to you, your loved ones, friends, your community and the world at large when your goal is achieved. The more you can think of, the greater the pulling power of your goal.

Include plenty of benefits to you personally. What would achieving this do for *you*? How would *your* life be better? What sort of person would it make you?

On the back of the sheet you may find it helpful to write down all the reasons why it's important that you do not fail, and anything that you want to eliminate from your life which will be gone when you achieve your goal, such as loneliness, financial hardship, boredom, excess weight, etc.

Everyone is motivated to some extent both by moving *towards* what they want and moving *away from* what they don't. You mustn't dwell on failure, but a realistic assessment of the consequences of not succeeding can help concentrate the mind.

51

List the intermediate steps, the stepping stones on the way to your goal, with the dates by which you intend to achieve them. You need long-, medium- and short-term goals. Some of your medium- and short-term goals are like milestones towards your long-term goals; the remainder stand on their own, some important in their own right, some for fun.

Think of achieving your ambitions as climbing a ladder:

■ What's at the top?

■ What must you do to reach the top?

■ What is the first step? Write it down and commit to taking this step right now.

■ What's the next step?

■ The one after that?

■ Where do you want to be five years from today?

■ What is your priority for the next 12 months? Three months? Next month?

You need lots of short-term goals so you're able to continually assess your progress towards your longer-term goals.

52

Identify the support or infrastructure required to achieve your goal. This could include other people whose skills, knowledge and practical assistance you need to access, financial and material resources, organisations you need to tap into, etc.

Many goals require support from other people or organisations. Who might these be? Who will help you achieve your goal? You'll need people to complement your own skills and contacts who can provide information and practical assistance. Can you anticipate your support needs? Where will you look for it?

It may help to assemble support material for your main goals – news articles, books, tapes, videos/DVDs, magazine articles, websites, lists of useful contacts, etc. Review these often.

53

How will you know when you've achieved your goal? What are the key performance indicators? Are they observable, measurable?

Close your eyes and imagine you have already done it – how is life different? What does it look like? What does it feel like? Sound like? Use the senses to pull it closer. Hold on to this feeling for a few moments. Then open your eyes and write down anything that comes to you.

Visualise your goal as reality every day. Make it real in your imagination, and you *will* make it real in your life (see pages 103–105).

54

To strengthen your commitment, sign up for your goal on the dotted line, date it, and set a date for review one to six months hence, depending on the allotted timescale. Write the review date on your wall chart.

Review your short-term goals every week, your medium-term goals monthly and long-term goals at least every six months. Also, check that your short- and medium-term goals are still consistent with your primary goal.

55

Now write your main goals down on a small card. Keep it in your wallet or purse and carry it around with you. Read them through first thing in the morning and last thing at night. Read them aloud. Read them frequently to keep them at the forefront of your mind. Not only does this help impress them on your subconscious autopilot, it also reminds you of the actions that you must take to move you closer to their completion.

Goals: some more dos and don'ts

The following tips make your goals more specific, more motivating and more easily achievable.

56

Start by identifying your primary goal. This goal will define the direction of your life and be closely related to your values and mission. Then write down your subsidiary goals.

Free your imagination – don't worry about the 'how' part at this stage, just be totally honest about what you want from your life.

Don't make your goals list too long at first. If you try to achieve too many things at once you may diffuse your endeavours and end up accomplishing very little.

57

You may have to be prepared to specialise if your main goal is an ambitious one, at least for a year or two. Every one of us has the ability to attain excellence or make an outstanding contribution at something, but if you want to be a great musician it's unlikely that you'll also have the time to become a great athlete. It's possible, but improbable.

To do yourself justice you may have to channel most of your energies towards one major goal for a while. If you're studying for some important examinations in six months, it is perfectly reasonable to give it most of your time and attention. But be clear on how long you intend this phase of your life to be.

58

Set some lesser goals that are relatively easy to accomplish. This reinforces the goal setting habit and gives you encouragement. Not all your goals need to be momentous. Minor goals, like solving a crossword puzzle or finishing a task in time to watch a favourite TV programme, are the stuff of our daily lives, but by themselves are not life-changing. You also need goals that stretch and challenge you. Above all, your goals must excite you. When you examine your list of goals, do you have a feeling of excitement in your stomach? If so, good! You're on the right lines.

59

If you find it easier to come up with 'don't wants' than 'wants', turn them around. For example, your internal dialogue may go something like this:

'I need a job, but I don't want to work in an office.'
'OK, so would you like to work behind a bar?
'Not likely.'
'In a shop?'
'No.'
'A factory?'
'Absolutely not.'
'Would you like to work outdoors?'
'Not really. But I would like to have a job that involves travel.'
'What would be your ideal travel job?'

And so on.

60

Don't try to set goals on other's behalf, for example:

■ I want my son to go to university.

■ I want my children to be interested in music.

■ I want my parents to accept me as I am.

■ I want my friends to realise what a special person I am.

■ I want my daughter to train as a nurse.

Only the individuals concerned are qualified to set these goals, because only they can make them happen.

61

Be specific. What exactly do you want? How much of it? Where do you want it, when, in which situations?

Avoid nebulous words and phrases like 'I want to help people'. Exactly how do you want to help them? It's no use writing that you want to be happier (or healthier, or richer, or more popular, etc): what does this mean for you in detail? If your goal is to acquire a material object, be precise. What make and model will that new car be? How many rooms will your dream house have, and what about a garage, garden and conservatory? If you want a better job, what specifically does 'better' mean? More money (if so, how much?), more fun, more freedom, meeting more people, more travel, more time outdoors?

Here are some examples:

- My goal is to earn £x thousand a year by the end of the year 2....

- My aim is to pass my exams this summer with distinction.

- My goal is to win the tennis club championship this year.

- It is 31 July, and I own a new BMW 6 Series.

- My goal is to shed 20lb by 30 June so my weight is no more than 12 stone.

- My goal is to contact 20 organisations in South America and get myself invited on a lecture tour.

62

Think carefully before you settle on your final list. Are your goals sufficiently challenging? Are there any negative consequences of achieving a goal, and can you live with them? Are you being fair to yourself? Also, remember your goals must include basic personality and lifestyle changes; without them you won't achieve any of your other goals.

63

Don't try to identify all your goals at once. Keep coming back to them and be willing to update your list. Once you've started the process ideas will keep popping into your head. Spend time in contemplation. Are they really what you want? Do they provide the fulfilment, the excitement and enjoyment you seek? Fine-tune your list to make sure you have only written down things you really desire.

The big test of whether a goal is right for you is to ask yourself, 'If I could have this right now, would I take it?' If the answer is an unequivocal 'yes', eureka!

64

Don't shirk a challenge; pretending you don't want something just because it's difficult to get is self-defeating. Remember the tale of the fox and the grapes? The fox couldn't reach the grapes, so he convinced himself they were sour.

Don't be like the fox. Accept that you want your goals realised and don't have them, but don't decry them. There's a price to be paid for living your dream – the time, effort and, yes, occasionally hardship and inconvenience. How much time and effort are you prepared to commit to getting what you most want from life? If you've identified the right goals, any sacrifices are worth it.

65

Choose your own goals. This may seem obvious, but many people fall into the trap of doing what is expected of them. They try to live up to their parents' expectations, or match someone else's achievements rather than focusing on what is right for them.

Sir Viv Richards, the West Indian cricketing legend, did not make this mistake. As a youngster he lived and breathed sport. His talent was so obvious, his headmaster turned a blind eye to his neglected schoolwork and allowed him to concentrate on cricket. However, his father saw his son's sporting obsession as a distraction and did everything in his power to steer him into a 'proper' job.

If Sir Viv had gone along with his father's wishes, would he have been as successful? Unlikely. Would he have been as happy? Not a chance. If you allow someone else to set your goals, the inner drive isn't there. So choose your goals for yourself and commit yourself to them wholeheartedly.

66

Make your short-term goals demanding but realistic. Short- and medium-term goals are only effective as motivators if they you think they are attainable within your chosen timescale. Short-term goals should be ten to 20 per cent beyond your current state, challenging but within reach. To move each goal along, take a few moments every Sunday evening to think about what you can do in the next seven days.

67

To stay on track:

- Buy a wall chart/calendar and plot your short- and medium-term goals on the target dates.

- Use a desk-top calendar and set your goals for next month.

- Use a pocket week-at-a-glance type diary to remind yourself of the main activities for the next seven days.

68

When you have specified a goal, think about the first step you need to take. Write it down.

Commit to taking this first step now. Do something today to get started. Make a call, set up a meeting, think about the resources you need, start investigating the options, talk to someone who can help you, whatever you need to do. After that, take action every day, refusing to hesitate, doubt or give in.

69

Update your list on a regular basis. What you wanted five or even two years ago might not be what you want at present. Circumstances change – children grow up, companies reorganise, problems arise and are solved, relationships change.

Critically review your major goals and your plans annually (31 December is a good day – make your New Year's resolutions really count for something). Make any changes that are appropriate. It will become obvious when a goal no longer has any attraction for you, so drop it. Goal setting is not supposed to be so rigid and inflexible that you can't make alterations, but don't change a goal just because it seems too difficult. No one ever built a better life by copping out.

70

Keep your goals confidential, or, if you must, share them only with like-minded individuals who have goals of their own or people who can help you.

Many people are quite derisive about anyone who has dreams and ambitions, which can be very disheartening, especially if things aren't going well.

71

Before you settle on your final list, make sure your goals are reasonably balanced and complementary. Make sure that you are not paying too much attention to, say, your social life at the expense of your career or family. Lopsided goals usually result in problems in the neglected areas.

Also make sure that your goals are, for you, physically possible. For example, if you have not exercised regularly for a while, have yourself checked out by a doctor before commencing on an exercise programme.

Work-life balance

It's important to get the work-life balance right. Work is an important part of life, but it should never take over.

If you love your work and get on well with your colleagues you are indeed fortunate, but what if you don't? For many people work is just a drudge, with no real satisfaction other than the pay. Sadly, only a small percentage of people truly love what they do and gain genuine satisfaction from it.

If you are unhappy with your work-life balance you need to review your working life and decide whether it's time to make changes. Everyone has the potential to earn a living doing something they enjoy – if they go about it the right way.

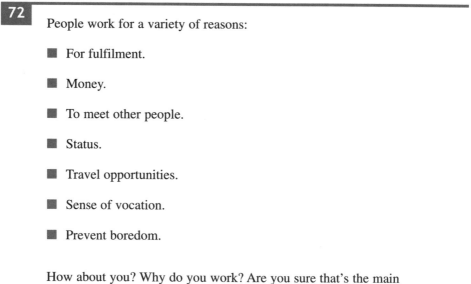

72

People work for a variety of reasons:

- For fulfilment.

- Money.

- To meet other people.

- Status.

- Travel opportunities.

- Sense of vocation.

- Prevent boredom.

How about you? Why do you work? Are you sure that's the main reason? At times when you feel frustrated or irritated with an aspect of your work, do you maintain a deep feeling that what you're doing is right for you?

73

If you are gainfully employed, how do you feel about your work?

■ Do you find it easy to go to work most days?

■ What do you like about your job? Hate about it?

■ How stressed do you feel at work?

■ What do you get out of it?

■ Do you need to earn more, but don't know how?

If you are not working, how do you feel about that? Would you like to work? What would you ideally like to do?

74

Imagine your ideal job.

■ What would the work entail?

■ Do you want to work full-time or part-time? Regular hours or flexible hours?

■ How do you feel about working in a team or managing others?

■ What level of salary and benefits would you want?

■ Would you prefer to be employed or self-employed?

■ Would home working suit you?

■ What qualifications, experience and personal qualities would you need to do that job?

■ Are you prepared to move for work? Are you willing to commute?

■ How far would you move for the right opportunity? Would you like to work abroad?

Write down your thoughts.

75

Imagine you are applying for your ideal job. Prepare a letter of application and a CV. If you were interviewing for this ideal job, would you offer it to yourself? If not, why not? What new skills, character traits, qualifications and experience do you need?

Step one: summing up

Setting challenging yet realistic goals consistent with your talents, values and interests is the starting point of a fulfilling life filled with happiness and success. Long-term goals give you a much needed sense of purpose and direction. Medium-term goals bring them within sight. Short-term goals keep the momentum going and enable you to fill your days with meaningful, useful activity. Very few people are happy to be aimless and unoccupied.

Clear goals keep you focused, allow you to take decisions more easily, make full use of your energy, your talents and proclivities, help you plan your time more effectively and enable you to accomplish far more. They are the means by which you create your future, rather than the future creating you.

I'm often asked whether it is healthy to be obsessed with goals. I answer that choosing goals is not about being obsessed, although you must bear in mind if you want to achieve at a high level, that outstandingly successful individuals are usually passionate about what they are doing. You don't have to be *obsessed* with goals, rather use them to clarify what you want out of life and progress steadily towards them, enjoying what you're doing and keeping your life in balance.

3 Step Two: Using The Awesome Power Of Your Mind

> *The vast majority of people are born, grow up, struggle, and go though life in misery and failure, not realising that it would be just as easy to switch over and get exactly what they want out of life, not recognising that the mind attracts the thing it dwells upon.*
>
> **Dr Napolean Hill**

Your mind is your greatest asset. There is a magnetic force generated within you which draws you to whatever your mind centres upon. As your mindpower develops, so does this magnetic force, attracting conditions and people that promote success.

One of the main causes of failure is not cultivating the power of the mind, but this won't be a problem for you if you apply the powerful techniques on the next few pages.

The Law of Attraction

76

The Law of Attraction states that whatever we focus our attention on and think about most often, we attract into our lives. We create events and circumstances into our lives according to our dominant thoughts. Any line of thinking which we believe and on which we constantly dwell takes root in the subconscious and cannot fail to influence us.

When you place your attention on what you can't do, don't have and can't have, and mentally justify why you can't do or have them (which many people do), you act on what you can't do and can't have, and then, according to the Law of Attraction, they materialise in your life. On the other hand, when you fill your mind with happy, constructive and loving thoughts, you become happy, constructive and loving, and attract others of the same disposition and create the best possible circumstances for yourself.

We are each a walking manifestation of our predominant thoughts. For some this is rather frightening, but once you realise that you are the only person who can think your thoughts, and that you are in charge of your thoughts, it becomes exciting. You realise that, no matter what has gone before, you have the power to move in any direction you choose.

From now on, be very careful what you think about!

The ITIA formula

77

The key to using the full power of your mind is the ITIA formula. ITIA stands for:

Intention
Thought
Imagination
Action

1 Intention

■ What do you want out of life?

■ What kind of person would you like to be?

■ What changes would you like to make?

■ What are your goals?

■ Are you prepared to commit yourself?

The clearer your goals and the stronger your intentions, the more likely they are to be realised.

2 Change your way of thinking

Step back and observe your self-talk (your thoughts).

■ Are they generally positive or negative?

■ What questions do you ask yourself?

■ Examine your attitudes and beliefs. Where have they brought you so far?

■ What are you trying to achieve by thinking that way?

The more positive your thinking, the happier you are and the more likely to succeed.

3 Imagination

■ Learn to use your creative imagination and respect your intuition.

■ Imagine achieving your goals. What will they look like when brought to fruition? Sound like? Feel like?

■ Do this often, especially when you are physically and mentally relaxed.

■ Imprint your desires – and the belief that they will come true – on your subconscious mind.

4 Act 'as if'

■   Take small steps.

■   Ignore your discomfort – feel the fear and do it anyway.

■   Monitor your progress and make adjustments if necessary.

■   Keep going until it becomes a habit.

■   And don't be put off by others.

Change never feels right, but when you act 'as if', eventually the uncomfortable feelings fade away.

The ITIA formula takes into account everything known about the mind, how it processes information and brings about change. But you must do *all four*; otherwise the changes won't be permanent.

The power of thought

> *They can because they think they can.*
>
> **Virgil**

The Principle of Cause and Effect states that every action is a cause and every cause produces an effect. But what governs your actions? The answer is – your thoughts.

Every action begins with a thought. Constructive thoughts lead to constructive actions, foolish thoughts to foolish actions, destructive thoughts to destructive actions. Most human beings are severely limited by their thinking.

When you become aware of the effect your thoughts have on your life, you become very conscious of what you're thinking. You start to take control of your thoughts. Sometimes even small changes make a huge difference – for example, the difference between 'I can' and 'I can't' can be massive. Failure always starts with the thought, 'I can't'. The antidote for this paralysing 'can't' consciousness is the affirmation, 'I can'. Affirm it as often as you can.

How you manage your thoughts is under your control. Therefore, by choosing to think positively you can choose positive goals, positive words, positive actions and hence create positive conditions in your life.

78

Take a deep breath, close your eyes and relax.

In your mind's eye, examine the events and circumstances of your life. Don't judge, criticise or condemn.

Consider how your way of thinking has shaped your reality.

How have your beliefs affected your life?

How have your actions and habits created your life?

79

When we are thinking, we are talking to ourselves. This inner conversation is the 'internal dialogue' or **self-talk**. It is, in effect, the functioning of your conscious mind. The internal dialogue is conditioned by past experience and what we believe about ourselves and the world.

Obviously the most draining, tiresome and morale-destroying conversations we have with ourselves else are those which focus on our weaknesses, bad luck (real or imagined), failures and deficiencies. From now on, stop criticising yourself, and don't dwell on your 'faults'. Most of your so-called faults are simply programmed thinking patterns which fall away as you become more aware of yourself.

Make it a motto to never say anything about yourself, either silently or out loud, that you don't want to materialise in your life.

80

Ask yourself:

- How are my current thoughts, words and actions creating my future?

- Where is my predominant way of thinking leading me?

- Is it where I want to go?

Spend some time on this. It can be very instructive.

Turning your thinking around

81

Listening to your self-talk, emphasising the positive trains of thought and gently distancing yourself from the negatives is the starting point of turning your thinking around.

Every day you think around 50,000 thoughts. Most of these float up from the subconscious and are heavily conditioned by past experiences. You can't stop them, but you can decide what to do with them. If they are constructive to what you want, carry on thinking those thoughts. If not, let them go.

Fortunately, human beings are not like robots. We can decide what to do with our thoughts, but like any new skill, it takes practice. Once mastered, you'll find that the technique that follows becomes habitual. Within a few weeks, you'll just do it naturally.

The starting point is to accept that you are responsible for your thoughts and the words and actions that result. Then apply the following four steps.

Step one: be mindful

82 'Mindfulness' is simply being aware of your thoughts. You become more mindful by listening to your 'internal dialogue' or 'self-talk'.

Try this: stop what you are doing for a few moments. Be still and listen to your thoughts. Don't be too analytical or judgmental; simply register what is taking place. If your mind starts to wander, bring it back. Your mind will gradually quieten down and you'll gain a new insight into its workings.

Do this several times a day.

83 Once you have mastered the above exercise, start to frequently check on your level of positivity. Pause for a few moments every so often and ask yourself:

■ Did I just react negatively?

■ Have I reacted negatively at all today?

■ Am I focusing on solutions, not problems?

■ How can I improve?

Keep reminding yourself that positive thinking creates happiness and success.

84 Warning! As you become more self-aware, you may surprise yourself with just how ingenious you can become in creating excuses for hanging on to old thinking patterns.

Don't fall into the trap of believing that negative thinking is more realistic, or that if you started thinking positively you'd be lying to yourself, or your friends would go off you. None of these are true. Refuse to entertain such thoughts.

Step two: release disempowering thoughts

85

It's a fact that your conscious mind can only hold one thought at a time. This means that when you are dwelling on disempowering thoughts, you are blocking out empowering thoughts. Therefore the sooner you can let go of disempowering thoughts, the better.

Do this using the **thought stopping** technique. As soon as you become aware of an unwanted thought, say 'Stop!', 'Cancel!' or 'Go away!' Let it go. If you're on your own, do something physical like clapping your hands or stamping a foot, which immediately breaks the pattern. You can also imagine closing a book, a symbolic gesture that that's the end of it. Practise this until you can use it effortlessly at any time.

If you catch yourself thinking negatively, don't be angry with yourself – this would merely be exchanging one disempowering thought for another. Instead, just drop the thought and pat yourself on the back. Meet your thoughts with understanding; they're not harmful unless you dwell on them and believe them.

Very few individuals have ever been able to completely control their thoughts. Even when you practise this technique, disempowering thoughts will continue to float up from the subconscious, but over time they will become less frequent and have less effect.

86

A variant of thought stopping is the **rubber band technique**. This simple method works by increasing your awareness of your thoughts, emotions and behaviours, enabling you to release and replace those you don't want.

Wear a rubber band on your left (or right if you prefer) wrist, just above the watch band. When you become aware of an unwanted thought or habit, twang the rubber band. The slight pain sends a message to the brain and changes the way the thought or habit is wired into your nervous system.

For example:

- To stop smoking, twang the rubber band every time you think about a cigarette.

- To change a destructive emotion, e.g. anger or worry, twang the band every time you feel the emotion arising.

- Use it to change feeble thinking into purposeful thinking and 'problem thinking' into 'solution thinking'.

- Use it to pause and think before speaking out.

87

Worry is destructive thought. It influences what you do and how you do it. It can even affect your health; it is proven that hospital patients who constantly worry about their recovery get better more slowly.

One way to deal with worry is to start a worry box. Write down what's bothering you on a slip of paper, place it in the box, and turn your attention to something else.

On the last day of each month, open the box and examine the contents:

- Discard any that no longer need concern you.

- If you can do something to ease or resolve a worry, do it immediately.

- Place the rest back in the box.

You'll find over the months that 90 per cent of your worries are just foolish thoughts, utterly groundless.

Step three: turn your attention to some positive thoughts

88

Having released a thought, immediately turn your attention to a more affirmative one. The simplest substitute is its direct opposite, for example:

Change...	Into...
I can't	I can
I won't	I will
I'm stupid	I'm clever
I'm weak	I'm strong
I haven't	I have
I don't	I do
I'm ugly	I'm attractive

Don't worry it feels like you're lying to yourself. Your feelings are not reliable indicators when you are attempting any form of personal change. Think of this method as a tool to help you change your way of thinking rather than a literal statement of truth.

89

Alternatively, use an affirmation. Affirmations are planned self-suggestions which can be used for many purposes. For example:

■ To change negative attitudes into positives, e.g. 'I now release with ease all my old negative attitudes,' 'I think, talk and act positively at all times.'

■ To develop the qualities you need, e.g. 'I shall persist until I succeed,' 'I am determined, patient and courageous.'

■ To foster self-approval, e.g. 'I accept, love and approve of myself,' 'I deserve success. I have confidence in myself.'

■ To speed your personal growth, e.g. 'I am willing to change and to grow, and every day in every way I get better and better.'

Either compose an appropriate affirmation when you need one, or use a favourite 'off the shelf'.

90

Choose half a dozen affirmations that appeal to you from this list and memorise them.

■ Every day I keep my thoughts positive, because I am the result of what I think.

■ I always maintain a perfectly healthy body and mind.

■ I'm happy, healthy, wealthy and whole.

■ I only think about and visualise what I want to happen.

■ I have balance and harmony in my life.

■ No matter what has gone before, I now take charge of my life.

■ I can achieve whatever I set my mind to.

■ I can achieve anything I want, and if I apply myself and persist, I can do it.

■ I have all the personal qualities required to manage and motivate others.

■ I will persist until I succeed.

■ I am now reaching a place where every thought I have is loving and caring.

■ I am in radiant, vibrant, dynamic health.

■ I do it now in the most relaxed and efficient manner, with inner calmness and purposeful activity.

■ I feel warm and loving towards myself.

■ I am worthy of all the good in my life. I deserve the best.

■ I think, talk and act confidently at all times.

■ I believe in myself. I can do anything I choose.

■ I like myself.

■ I am a strong and worthy person.

■ I am cool, calm and in control.

■ I am successful in everything I do.

■ I am whole, perfect, strong, powerful, loving, harmonious, prosperous and happy.

You now have some 'off the shelf' affirmations that you can use whenever you need.

91

Making up your own affirmations: when composing your affirmations, there are certain rules you must observe for maximum effect.

■ *Personalise them*. Affirmations are powerful tools for changing yourself, but *your* affirmations cannot change other people or influence *their* behaviour.
The best way to make them personal to you is to start them with the pronoun, 'I'. For example, 'I accept, love and approve of myself'; 'I am determined, patient and persistent,'; 'I am calm, peaceful and relaxed.'

■ *Put them in the present tense*. This is important because the subconscious takes everything literally. If you were to use the future tense, it would assume that what you want is not an immediate priority.
Stating your affirmations in the present means, in practise, that most of your affirmations will begin with 'I am', 'I can', 'I have' or 'I do'.

■ *Use only positive words and phrases*. Otherwise, you might inadvertently end up with the opposite of what you intended. This is because the subconscious overlooks a negative word if it occurs in the middle of a sentence. For example, 'I do not fail' registers as 'I fail' and 'I am not fat' as 'I am fat'. Instead, affirm, 'I succeed' and 'I am slim'.

■ *Write them on small cards and carry them with you*. Use CAPITAL LETTERS (they have greater impact on your subconscious). Write them on post-it notes and stick them to your bathroom mirror, dashboard, fridge and other prominent places. Read them frequently throughout the day.

92

For this exercise, simply sit in silence and affirm what you desire. Close your eyes, take a deep breath and relax, think of your goals and affirm that you already have them. If you wish, incorporate statements such as:

■ I can be what I choose to be.

■ I can achieve whatever I set my mind to.

■ I believe in myself. I can do anything I choose.

93

Make up three or four affirmations targeted at current issues in your life. Use them for a month, following the above guidelines (91).

At the end of the month, review your progress. What changes have you noticed? In what ways do you feel different? How well have they worked for you?

94

Increasing the effectiveness of your affirmations:

■ Say your affirmations with feeling, whether silently or out loud. The greater the emotion, the better.

- Practise. Repetition works, so use your affirmations often. Last thing at night is the best time, because your subconscious mind is at its most receptive. Give it something uplifting to work on while you are asleep. First thing in the morning is also very beneficial.

- Suspend disbelief, especially if you are working towards something you don't yet have physically. Consider affirmations as tools for change and remember that you are in the early stages of creating something which will eventually materialise. The results may not be immediate, but if you have faith, they will come.

- Record them onto a cassette tape or minidisk and listen frequently, especially last thing at night.

- If your goal is something tangible, carry a photograph or a reminder with you (such as a small model or branded key ring if you are in the process of acquiring a new car). Affirm that it is yours every time you look at it. If you are skilled at digital photography and you can create a photograph of yourself holding that trophy or wearing that medal on your computer, do it, and hang a framed copy on your wall. Every time you see it, it reinforces the message to your subconscious autopilot.

95

Although you can use affirmations any time, they are most effective when you are in that dreamy, relaxed state known as **alpha level**. In alpha your subconscious is more receptive to new suggestions. This is called **autosuggestion**. Autosuggestion is a powerful tool for reprogramming the mind for success.

Alpha level (or the alpha state) is explained fully on page 92.

Step four: keep at it!

96

Learning any new skill takes practice and persistence, and this one is well worth acquiring.

It takes approximately four weeks to change a thinking habit using these techniques – that's not long to set yourself on a new, more satisfying course.

97

Become more aware of the effect people and events have on your thinking. Most people are unaware of how destructive negative thinking can be, and they don't realise they have it within their power to change. You may have to minimise your contact with the 'isn't it awfuls' and 'poor mes' until your new thinking habits are firmly installed.

Watch your language

Life coaches listen very carefully to the language you use – it gives all sorts of clues to your motivation, your attitudes and beliefs, self-image and relationship with others. A life coach would be quick to point out disempowering words and phrases, and encourage you to reflect upon and modify them.

The language you use when you talk to yourself is all-important, and there's much you can do to empower yourself through more uplifting self-talk.

98

As you become adept at turning your thinking around, you'll find you become very aware of disempowering words and phrases, and able to change them to lessen their impact. You soften negative phrases, or change mildly negative phrases to positives.

Here are some examples:

Change these disempowering words and phrases...	...to these softer words and phrases...	...or these positives
Angry	A bit upset	Calm/in control
Anxious	Concerned	Keyed up
Depressed	Feeling down	Happy/wonderful
Exhausted	Tired	Energised
Frightened	Bothered	Courageous
Guilty	Regretful	Blameless
Harassed	Busy	Relaxed
Inadequate	Unsure	Capable
Irritable	Unsettled	Calm
Lazy	Relaxed	Industrious
Pessimistic	Uncertain	Optimistic
Stressed	Slightly tense	Busy/occupied
Worried	Uneasy	Unconcerned

99

People use words differently, so jot down a few words that create painful feelings in you. Some of these may be the result of experiences you had as a child; a turn of phrase repeatedly used by an angry parent can leave a lasting impact.

Make a list of words and phrases you could use instead to lower their intensity. Substitute these for the old in your internal dialogue. What differences do you notice in the way you feel when you use these new expressions?

100

Just for today, notice how many times you use the following words, either aloud or silently to yourself:

Can't, don't, won't, couldn't, wouldn't

Each time you catch yourself using these words, change them to the opposite. How does it feel?

101

Replace 'try to' with 'will' in your vocabulary. 'Try' has built in excuses for failure. Focus on things you *intend* to do, rather than on things you mean to *try*. Think about it: if you invite a friend to a party and they say, 'I'll try to make it,' what does that suggest? Contrast this with 'Thank you, I'll definitely be there.'

102

Be aware of how often you use the following words and phrases, either aloud or to yourself:

Should, must, ought, have to, supposed to

These expressions often presuppose a set of rules or code of conduct that has been imposed on you (usually by a parent figure) rather than thought out and chosen for yourself. Change them to:

I choose, decide, want, prefer, like

These terms put you where you belong – firmly in the driving seat.

Ask the right questions

Was Socrates the first life coach? The Socratic method, which is still universally used as a teaching technique, consists of asking sequences of questions which challenge learners and make them think more deeply. This is how Socrates challenged the young men of Athens to reflect on the issues of the day. It brought about such profound changes in their attitudes and behaviour that he was adjudged by the authorities to be a threat to society and forced to drink hemlock, a deadly poison.

Hopefully no life coach would ever suffer the same fate for turning their clients' thinking around, for skilled, effective questioning is a potent tool in the hands of a good coach. In the same way, the quality of the questions you ask yourself and the way you ask them is key to your success as a self-coach.

Questions focus your attention. Great questions:

■ Shift your attention to a more positive, practical, upbeat perspective.

■ Presuppose a solution where none was previously apparent.

■ Open doors to new imaginative, creative and intuitive resources within your own mind.

■ Create clarity.

■ Are simple to answer.

■ Explore different perspectives and generate options.

■ Create forward movement, out of the problem state and into action.

■ Motivate.

■ Help you feel more in control and constructive about a situation.

■ Can make a problem feel more like a challenge or an opportunity.

■ Dig below the surface, and therefore invite a more encompassing solution.

■ Avoid unhelpful judgements.

■ Give direction to your self-talk and actions.

Poor questions confuse, lead you up blind alleys, narrow options, demotivate you, and lower your energy, confidence and self-esteem.

103 Sometimes the internal dialogue takes the form of a series of questions. 'What can I do next?' 'Why did I do that?' 'Why did they do that?' 'Why am I so stupid?' 'How come I always miss out?'

When you eavesdrop in on your self-talk, make a note of the sort of questions you ask yourself.

The subconscious mind

The mind has two levels, **conscious** and **subconscious**. The conscious mind is the thinking mind that reasons, debates and analyses.

The subconscious is the memory store for all the information received from the conscious mind. It has no intelligence. It does not have the ability to reason or analyse. It simply receives information from the conscious mind. A specific thought repeatedly presented to the subconscious influences the brain and muscular mechanisms of the body. Record-like grooves are formed in the subconscious, and the record is played over and over again as the thought becomes a habit.

When it receives information from the conscious, the subconscious accepts it as the whole and entire truth. It doesn't matter if the information is positive or negative, or even if it is true – it accepts the information as fact. Usually, nothing is received by the subconscious that has not been processed by the conscious for a length of time.

Receiving any suggestions as true, the subconscious at once proceeds to act on them. What the subconscious believes controls our behaviour and heavily influences what materialises in our lives. For example, continual thoughts of anger, bitterness, resentment, jealousy and so on are eventually absorbed by the subconscious. The effects are more often than not totally destructive.

The subconscious finds it very hard to accept new ideas, but when the censorious conscious mind is off guard, or when calm judgement is suspended (for instance, during wild excitement or panic), then the subconscious is left unguarded and open to suggestion from all sources.

Alternatively, as we shall see, the subconscious can be swayed by thoughts, feelings and images deliberately fed in when one is in a deeply relaxed state. (More of this from page 101.)

104

The subconscious mind is designed to come up with an answer to every question, even if the question is totally groundless or irrelevant.

Since it has no intelligence of its own, it can't challenge the validity of a question, only search its data banks for a response (usually drawn from your past experiences). It's like a computer – it does as it's told, even if what you're asking it to do makes no sense. It always tries to find an answer, regardless of the question.

A great question leads to a constructive answer. A poor question often leads to an unhelpful or damaging answer. This can make an already difficult situation even worse.

For example, if you ask yourself, 'Why am I so depressed', the subconscious takes it as read that you are depressed, even if you're just feeling a little low, and manufactures all the feelings associated with depression. Now you're on a downward spiral that may be hard to escape.

Likewise, if you ask yourself, 'How did I get into this awful mess', it homes in on 'mess', taking it as read that you are in an awful mess and that you did get yourself there, even if it's not that serious and due to events beyond your control. 'Because you're an idiot who never gets anything right,' it replies (or some other such nonsense). Before long, if this pattern repeats, you start to believe it and end up repeatedly sabotaging yourself.

Instead, ask for a solution. 'How can I handle this situation better?' 'What can I learn from this?' 'What seems important about this right now?' 'What can I do now to feel better?' All these questions presuppose a helpful answer. Now the subconscious homes in on 'handle better,' 'learn,' 'important,' and 'feel better now.' It has something positive to work on.

Make sure your questions direct you towards solutions rather than aggravate problems. You may not get an immediate answer, but if you're patient you will. The subconscious rarely works to deadlines and the answer may come when you least expect it, such as when you're mowing the lawn, washing up or driving to work.

Changing your problem statements into great questions

105

Learn to direct your questions towards finding solutions rather than mulling over problems. Make sure they presuppose a positive response and refocus your thoughts from problem to solution.

106

Closed questions are those that give up a short answer, such as yes, no or don't know. For example:

■ Would I be happy doing this job?

■ Is there a way to solve this problem?

■ What time is it?

■ Is this right for me?

■ Shall I ask her for a date?

■ Do I agree or disagree?

■ Am I asking the right question?

Closed questions can be helpful when you already have a list of options, but they are rather limiting. They rarely open your mind to new options and possibilities, nor access the more imaginative and intuitive resources within.

107

If the answer to a closed question is 'not sure,' 'can't say,' 'don't know', follow up with an open question, such as, 'Suppose I did know, then what would the answer be?' or 'Suppose I had a wise being within me who knows all the answers, what would he or she say?'

108

Open questions stimulate your thinking and produce a more detailed reply. They set in train the subconscious' creative thinking processes. (You are actually asking your intuition to guide you.)

The most useful open questions usually begin with:

- Who?

- How?

- What?

- Where?

- When?

For example:

- Who should I ask to help me with this problem?

- How can I best handle this situation?

- What are the pros and cons of applying for this job?

- What's the best way to ask her for a date?

- What am I willing to do to solve this problem?

- If there's one thing I could do differently, what would it be?

- Where should I look for an answer to this question?

- What can I learn from this?

- How can I make sure I don't make this mistake again?

- When would be the best time to go ahead with this project?

- What can I say to this person?

- What's the next step? The one after that? And then?

- What would be a better question to ask myself?

109 If your question doesn't move you forward, that is, you can't think of an answer, or the answer you get doesn't seem to work, ask yourself:

- How much more time do I need?

- Would it help to spend time in silent reflection?

- What other questions might help?

- Is there something else bothering me that needs to be addressed before I can proceed?

110 Write down three or four problems you are facing right now. For example:

- I'm not getting on very well with my partner.

- I'm lonely.

- I'm stuck in a job I hate, and I feel I'm going nowhere.

- Why can't I afford a holiday abroad like my neighbour?

Rephrase them into great questions. Write them down the left side of a piece of paper (or a page in your Self-Coaching Journal). Remember, great questions presuppose a solution, tap into your creative resources, generate alternatives, move you out of the problem state, and shift your attention to a more positive, practical point of view. For example:

- How can I explore the situation with my partner so we can find new, better ways of relating?

- What could I do to meet new people and make new friends?

- How can I find a new job, that I would enjoy and would give me the prospect of a better future?

- What would it take for me to have a holiday abroad this year?

111
Now answer your own questions. Focus on each question one at a time and write down any ideas or solutions that come to you on the right hand side of the page.

When you've thought of a range of options, choose which ones to commit to, and complete a goals pro-forma (1, pages 6–7). Follow the TGROW method through (pages 3–5) and put your plan into action.

Beliefs

> " *We often become what we believe ourselves to be. If I believe I cannot do something, it makes me incapable of doing it. When I believe I can, I acquire the ability to do it even if I didn't have it in the beginning.*
>
> **Mahatma Gandhi** "

Life coaches listen very carefully to their clients to get a clear understanding of their attitudes and beliefs. They know that empowering beliefs and a positive mental attitude are essential for success in any area of life. People who are generally optimistic, proactive and confident are considerably more likely to be successful at whatever they choose, and happier too.

Many cling to their beliefs long after they have ceased to make any rational sense. Well into the twentieth century there were still people arguing that the Earth is flat despite the irrefutable evidence to the contrary. The Flat Earth Society was only disbanded in the 1980s, 20 years after the Apollo moon landings had proved conclusively that our planet is a globe.

Beliefs affect us whether they are true or false. None of us deal with reality. We each deal with our own unique perceptions, our own understanding of truth, which may be deeply flawed.

If we believe we cannot do any better, we are in danger of underachieving simply because we don't believe we can improve and progress. We are inescapably held back by our limiting beliefs about ourselves, whatever the reality. That's why it's so important to get our beliefs working for, not against, us. So if you are aware of an unsupportive belief, let it go, give it up.

112

Consider:

- Do you believe in yourself?

- Do you have faith in your abilities?

- How much do you believe in yourself? Rate yourself on a scale of zero to ten (where zero means 'not at all' and ten means 'totally and completely'). If less than ten, why do you think that is?

- Do you believe you create your own circumstances? Or that life is something that happens to you?

113

Do you believe absolutely and with no doubt that you have the ability to accomplish your goals? All of them?

If not, take a pen and paper and make a few notes on how your life would be different if you really believed in yourself.

Never forget, when you believe in yourself, anything is possible.

114

What are beliefs? A belief is any collection of thoughts or ideas that you accept as true. Your beliefs are feelings of certainty about something.

Many of our beliefs are never questioned, yet form the basis of how we live our lives. The strongest beliefs usually concern 'the way it is', religion and other moral values such as respect for law and order, one's country and family responsibilities.

In which areas of your life do you hold the strongest beliefs?

115

Where do beliefs come from? Beliefs are learned; initially you acquired them from the people who raised you and those you grew up with, especially your parents, siblings, teachers and peer group. As you matured, you acquired more knowledge and began to interpret your experiences for yourself. All this had a powerful effect.

Beliefs are stored in the subconscious and constantly influence you. You normally think and act in accordance with your beliefs. When you don't, you feel profoundly uncomfortable.

Of course, some beliefs are more credible than others, but many are nothing more than unsubstantiated prejudices which have built up over the years and have little or no evidence to support them. A person whose parents repeatedly told them they're no good and will never amount to anything, for instance, is unlikely to have high self-esteem. Some of those who suffered from such comments manage to ignore them, but most can't. They are so ingrained in their subconscious that these poor souls live well below their true potential.

Whatever your experiences as a child, as an adult you can choose at any time to reject a discredited belief and believe something new, something different. You can consciously and deliberately create new beliefs; you can also change a belief you no longer want. Since beliefs are learned, and anything which is learned and can be unlearned and relearned, with a little determination you can replace any belief with a more empowering one. Then, as soon as you make the change and it is accepted by your subconscious, all the incoming evidence supports your new belief.

The hardest thing about changing a belief, ironically, is believing it's possible. People usually see their current beliefs as hard facts, how things are, unalterable. Some even think it commendable to die for their beliefs (and murder others in the process).

Think of someone you know, have read about or seen on film or TV who changed a belief about themselves. What effect did it have on their lives?

116

If you want evidence of how influential a belief can be, consider placebos – pills and potions containing no active ingredients. In healing, beliefs can be crucial to recovery because they deliver a direct command to the immune system. Author Norman Cousins (who cured himself of a terminal illness after doctors had given up on him) wrote, 'Drugs are not always necessary. Belief in recovery always is.'

Patients who are given placebos often make a full recovery. In her book *Positive Thinking*, Vera Peiffer gives two remarkable examples:

- When an antidepressant drug was tested experimentally, group A showed a success rate of 70 per cent, but those in group B, who had received a placebo, also showed a 70 per cent success rate. This is not unusual: there are literally thousands of well documented examples ranging from headache relief to cures for cancer, insomnia and heart disease.

- Even more incredible is the case of a convicted murderer in the United States who chose to have his wrists cut rather than go to the electric chair. The prisoner was blindfolded, and strapped to a chair. A warden traced across his wrists with a feather. He died instantly.

117

To what extent do your beliefs contribute to your happiness, contentment and wellbeing?

118

Ask yourself: what one, two or three things could I believe right now that would take me closer to my achieving my goal(s)?

> *Do not believe something just because wise men say so. Do not believe something just because it has always been that way. Do not believe something just because others may believe so. Examine and experience yourself.*
>
> **The Buddha**

Changing a belief

119

One of the most inspiring examples of an individual who challenged traditional beliefs is Roger Bannister. Before he ran the world's first sub four minute mile in 1954, the conventional wisdom was that human beings were not meant to run at this speed – the heart would burst under the strain. Then, with this belief shown up as false, within a year 37 other runners had done it too, followed within three years by another 300. Now thousands have run a sub four minute mile with no long term ill effects.

Note: dozens of athletes could have done what Bannister did; they were just as capable *physically*. Only their *beliefs* held them back.

120

Before you can get rid of your limiting beliefs, you must become aware of their existence. As they are largely subconscious, this is often easier said than done.

The most damaging belief is that you are the way you are, it is fixed and cannot change. But the most important attributes of successful people – confidence, a positive attitude, courage and determination and so on – are learned through experience.

Write down six limiting beliefs about yourself in the left hand column below, such as I'm too shy, I'm over the hill, it's too late to change, I'm not clever enough, I'm too hard on myself, etc. If there isn't enough room, continue on a separate sheet.

Then write in the right hand column what you would like to believe instead of these disempowering beliefs.

Some limiting beliefs about myself	What I would like to believe instead
1	
2	
3	
4	
5	
6	

121 Write down six beliefs about other people that you would like to change in the left hand column below, e.g. people are mostly selfish, they're only out for themselves, you only get rich by being mean, most people are better than me, etc.

Now write down what you would like to believe instead in the right hand column. By all means continue on a separate sheet if six isn't enough.

Some limiting beliefs about other people	What I would like to believe instead
1	
2	
3	
4	
5	
6	

122

Write in the left hand column below six beliefs about the world in general and how life is that you would like to change, e.g. life is hard, if you want something you've got to fight for it, we're not here to be happy, you have to be ruthless to succeed, etc, etc.

Now write in the right hand column what you would like to believe instead. (Continue on a separate sheet if six isn't enough.)

Some limiting beliefs about the world in general and how life is	What I would like to believe instead
1	
2	
3	
4	
5	
6	

You now have plenty of material to work on in the next few pages.

Disputing

123

One way to change a belief is to use a technique known as **disputing**. Disputing involves examining a belief in detail, pulling it apart, looking for evidence and challenging it using questions such as:

- Is it true?

- Where's the evidence?

- Do I believe this because I've thought it through myself, or because someone told me?

- Has it been built on the remarks of people in my early life, such as my parents, siblings, teachers, peer group, media figures, etc?

- How sure am I I've got it right?

■ What will be the long-term cost if I don't give up this belief?

■ What will be the long-term benefits of letting go of this belief?

■ What alternative belief(s) would serve me better?

124

Take the beliefs you identified in 120 to 122.

■ Examine each belief and dispute it using the questions in 123.

■ Then quickly write six endings for each of these sentences:
If this belief were really true...
If this belief turned out to be false...

You'll find this a very liberating experience.

Inquiry

125

A second way of challenging a redundant belief is to use Byron Katie's method, which she labels 'inquiry'. Her book *Loving What Is* is essential reading for anyone intending to move forward in their lives but finding themselves held back by restrictive beliefs.

Byron Katie claims that the main cause of unhappiness is allowing our thoughts to argue with reality. Wanting other people or the world to be different to how they are, she points out, is like trying to teach a cat to bark – stressful, frustrating and futile.

Thoughts which argue with reality are often characterised by the words 'should' and 'shouldn't'.

■ 'It shouldn't be allowed.'

■ 'People should be kinder to each other.'

■ 'Children should have more respect for their elders.'

■ 'Life should be fairer.'

■ 'People shouldn't smoke.'

■ 'They (politicians, the authorities, etc) should do something about it.'

What do all these sentences have in common? They're all hoping someone else changes, and who says they should? Wouldn't it be better to focus your attention on things you *can* change – your own attitudes and beliefs, actions and words – rather than those you *can't*?

126

The inquiry method involves:

1   Writing down the belief into which you wish to inquire.

2   Asking these four questions:
    • Is it true?
    • Can you absolutely know that it's true?
    • How do you react when you think that thought?
    • Who would you be without the thought?

3   Turning it around.
    • If your belief involves another person, put your own name instead of theirs.
    • Or try the extreme opposite – e.g. turn should into shouldn't.

Example

Belief: 'I got passed over for promotion yet again. My boss obviously doesn't like me.'

The four questions:

1   Is it true that your boss doesn't like you? (You probably think the answer is 'yes', but is there any evidence? What have they said or done that gives you that impression?)

2   Can you absolutely know that it's true? (Can you ever get inside the head of another human being and read their thoughts? Is there an implied 'should' in your thinking, i.e. 'my boss *should* like me'?)

3   How do you react when you think that thought? Happy? Optimistic?

I bet you don't. Can you see a reason to drop the thought? Can you find a stress-free reason to keep the thought? Is the reason peaceful, or stressful? (Hanging on to a belief that argues with reality is always stressful. It muddies your thinking and reduces your efficiency.)

4   Who (or what) would you be without the thought? (Usually more contented, more peaceful and more capable.)

Turn the underlying belief around. For example:

■ Turn it around to yourself (e.g. I don't like myself).

■ Turn it around to the other person (e.g. I should like my boss).

■ Turn it around to the opposite (e.g. my boss shouldn't like me unless they do).

The turnaround is not intended to be a literal statement of truth, but an alternative way of looking at the belief which may throw some interesting new light on the matter. Perhaps you were passed over for promotion because there were others more suitable, your boss sensed that you didn't like them and responded, or because you've been underperforming. Now you're getting down to the real cause, which you can do something to rectify.

127

Take the limiting beliefs you identified in 120–122 and apply the inquiry method.

Then ask yourself:

■ How do you feel about these beliefs now?

■ What does this tell you about yourself?

Developing a positive mental attitude

> *Nothing can stop a man with the right mental attitude from achieving his goal.*
> *Nothing on earth can help a man with the wrong mental attitude.*
>
> **Thomas Jefferson**

When a belief is expressed in words or actions, with emotion, it becomes an attitude.

Many studies have tried to find the secret of success and franchise it for commercial use, and contrary to what most people think, it is not the most gifted or even the hardest working who make it. The only consistent personality trait associated with success is a *positive attitude*.

When you approach a task with a positive attitude you feel more alive, more enthusiastic and more committed. You improve your chances of success immeasurably. Just as life coaches work on the attitudes of their clients, one of your principal aims in self-coaching is to cultivate positive attitudes, because you're unlikely to get far without them.

128

You already have the key to attitude change – the ITIA formula.

1   Clarify your intentions and set goals. Which attitudes would you like to drop? Which do you intend to develop?

2   Change your way of thinking. Be aware of your self-talk, the questions you ask yourself and your fundamental beliefs. What will you say to yourself now you have a new attitude? How will it be different?

3   Make full use of your creative imagination and intuition (see from page 89). Imagine what it is like to have a totally positive attitude. Imagine the difference it would make to your life. Imprint your new attitudes on your subconscious mind.

4   Act as if your new attitudes are already part of you. Behaviour reinforces the mental change. Overcome any idea that you can't do a thing by simply starting to do it, then keep on doing it until it becomes a habit.

These four steps reinforce each other, providing you do all four and keep at it.

129

Taking control: you can do little to change your gender, your race, your age, your height, the colour of your eyes, your shoe size and so on... but you can change your attitude to these and your way of dealing with any prejudice in others.

You have limited possibilities of transforming society generally, the government, your company/organisation (unless you own it!), and the way others (including your nearest and dearest) behave... but you can change your attitude to these, by updating your information about them and being alert to changes.

You cannot change the past... but you can change your attitude to it, including your childhood experiences, past successes, failures and misfortunes by seeing them as valuable opportunities for learning and growth.

130

Answer honestly:

1　Are you usually optimistic? Do you usually expect things to work out well?

2　Or are you a pessimist?

3　Do you usually expect the best of other people?

4　How do you react when things go badly?

5　How do you react when things go well?

6　Do you tend to blame 'bad luck' or others for your misfortunes?

7　Do you generally like other people?

8　Do you resent people who are more successful than you?

131

Ten empowering attitudes and beliefs:

1　I am responsible for my actions and creating the results I want in my life.

2　I am confident without being arrogant or aggressive.

3　I look for the good in every situation.

4　I am the sort of person who always finds a way through.

5　I have a strong belief in my own purpose.

6　I like people.

7　Life is here to be enjoyed.

8　Good people like me can succeed and be prosperous.

9　I am grateful for all the good in my life.

10　I'm good enough to have the life I want. I deserve to be happy.

Make a plan for instilling these attitudes and beliefs into yourself.

132

No matter how hard we try, we are all influenced by our environment. Others' attitudes rub off on us, and it's impossible to maintain an upbeat, affirmative attitude if you are constantly around people who are the opposite. Books, TV programmes and even the type of music we listen to all have an effect.

Get into the habit of mixing with go ahead, successful people. Choose optimistic friends, read uplifting books, listen to motivational audio programmes and seek out joyful, inspirational movies.

Great expectations

Your **expectations** are among your most influential beliefs. Clinical research backs up the conclusion that low expectations bring poor results and high expectations bring great results.

Many studies have shown that children of average ability taught by teachers with high expectations outperform groups of children of equal ability taught by teachers with low expectations. Raising children's expectations undoubtedly raises their level of achievement. Moreover, children with high achieving parents are likely to follow suit, because of the positive expectation (as long as it is not too pressured) they receive from their parents.

Expectations have a powerful effect on our aspirations, performance, achievements, relationships and on who we become. Expecting to fail is like tackling your goals with both hands tied behind your back. But if you expect to succeed, you're already on your way.

Open your mind to all life's possibilities. If you expect the best, you'll probably get it!

133

The three types of expectation that most affect our lives are:

1   Those our parents had (or have – it's not unusual for people in middle age to be still governed by their parents' expectations) of us, which can have a dramatic effect on how we feel about ourselves today. Many successful people would not have achieved what they did if they'd been swayed by the run of the mill expectations their parents had of them.

2   Those we have of others, especially our children and friends and colleagues who look up to us. They can be very sensitive to our expectations of them.

3   The expectations we have of ourselves. Some people believe it's better to expect less, then they won't be disappointed. These people usually under-achieve and it's not difficult to see why.

Make a list of expectations that have shaped your life. Can you identify where they came from? Did they restrict or broaden you? Spend some time on this – bringing negative expectations out into the open helps you work them through and turn them around.

134

Think of a recent situation where your negative expectations came true. What happened? What could you have done differently?

135

Think of something you have attempted recently where results didn't come up to your expectations.

Why was this? Was it because your expectations were too high? What could you have done to change the result?

Now think of something you have attempted recently where results were excellent. Why was this? What did you do differently? If you had taken the same approach to the first task (where results were disappointing) what effect would this have had on the outcome?

136 Create a new habit: expect the best each day. Programme your mind from the moment you awake with positive thoughts and mental images. Be mindful of your every waking expectation.

Remind yourself that what you do and say helps shape your expectations. Focus your attention on what you want and affirm that you have it. And never, never give up.

Case study

St Peter's School in Paddington, a run-down area of London, used to be a place where pupils spat and swore at the teachers, truancy was rife and staff couldn't wait to leave. One class had 25 different teachers in one term. The building was squalid, and closure was imminent, because the school inspectors considered it a danger to pupils.

Then a determined young teacher arrived. Helen Ridding was from a privileged background, having attended a fee-paying boarding school, and was only 24.

Soon after she started, the Head suffered a breakdown and left her in charge. She could easily have moved on to a well-run school in a more pleasant part of the country, but Helen was made of sterner stuff. She was consumed with such passion over the plight of those young people that she decided to stay and fight.

Now, more than a decade later, St Peters is rated one of the best schools in the country. Pupils consistently attain at a level far above the national average, and visitors are struck by the confidence and commitment of the children. 'We aim high here,' asserts Helen. 'When expectations are high, children surprise you.'

Use your intuition

Intuition is a powerful 'knowing' widely experienced by successful people from all walks of life.

Have you ever felt an overpowering urge to do something without being able to explain it logically? Have you ever known, just *known* that something is right without being able to put it into words? If so, this was your intuition at work.

Intuition is available to everyone – and you are no exception.

137

How well developed are your intuitive powers?

1   Have you ever guessed what was in a letter before opening it, and been proved right?

2   Are you good at guessing games?

3   Do you accurately weigh up people when you meet them for the first time?

4   Do you instinctively know when something is going to work or not?

5   Do you ever wake up with the answer to something that has been bothering you?

Answer 'yes' to more than three of these questions, and your intuition is already highly developed, but don't worry if you scored less than this – your intuitive powers are there, waiting to be developed. You probably don't yet fully trust them.

138

To fully understand intuition, it is necessary to understand something of the workings of the brain. The brain has two hemispheres, left and right, connected by a network of tissue known as the *corpus callosum*. In broad terms, left brain activity is related to logical thinking and intelligence, and right brain activity to intuition, inspiration and emotion.

Some characteristics of the two hemispheres are shown below:

The left hemisphere	The right hemisphere
Deals with information in a logical order.	Can store and handle large amounts of information at once.
Can only deal with one item at a time.	Deals with wholes, not details.
Thinks in words. Controls verbal expression, grammar and use of language.	Thinks in pictures.
Controls mathematical functioning.	Responsible for creative achievements such as drawing and painting, music, design, etc.
Analyses, evaluates, judges, criticises.	Responsible for intuition, spontaneity, inspiration and emotions.
Special memory for recognising words and numbers.	Special memory for recognising people, objects and experiences.

Most people have a tendency to favour one side or the other, but much of the time we alternate between the two – women more so than men.

Coming up with new ideas is mainly a right brain function; evaluating and developing these ideas is a left brain task. Sometimes (e.g. creative writing, composing music, painting) you switch between left and right brains so quickly that you cannot tell which is being used. We usually receive only the germ of an idea from the right brain and have to use our left to develop it and bring it to fruition. When both sides are working in harmony, your brain is operating at its optimum.

139

Study the list of left and right brain characteristics above. With which are you more comfortable – left brain activity? Right brain activity? Both equally? Or not sure?

If you are predominantly left-brained, spend more time on activities which utilise the right brain. Choose something you enjoy – painting, drawing, dancing, music, walking in the country, or play games like Pictionary, Guesstures, etc. While doing so, stay focused on the present moment and avoid analytical thoughts.

If predominantly right-brained, spend more time on activities that develop the left brain. Play word games like Lexicon or Scrabble, and numbers and logic games like bridge, Monopoly, backgammon and chess.

140

Developing your intuition: your intuitive and creative facilities are housed in the brain's right hemisphere. You can access them by learning to control the pattern of your brain waves, which is achieved by relaxing the physical body and calming the mind.

Scientists have defined four areas of brain wave activity. In the normal waking state the brain vibrates at between 14 and 40 cycles per second (cps). This is the **beta state**. The average alert person produces brain waves at around 20 cps, but it can increase to 25 or more if the person is emotionally aroused. Excessive levels of brain activity can produce over-excitability, poor concentration and feelings of panic.

Between 8 and 13 cps is a zone of relaxation, a dreamy state on the boundary of waking and sleeping. This is the **alpha level**. Here, the two halves of the brain are in equilibrium. Most people learn to experience this with their eyes closed.

When we enjoy a deep, comfortable sleep, the brain's activity slows to 5–7 cps (**theta state**). Below this is the **delta state**, the zone of total unconsciousness (coma).

The most important of these is the alpha state. Here, you can deliberately and effectively influence your subconscious thinking patterns and access your creative potential. Achieving this restful state is an invaluable skill. The key is spending regular time in relaxation.

141

Deep relaxation: the ability to relax can be learned quickly and easily. Here is a quick and simple method. (If you have difficulty relaxing, I suggest you purchase one of the many excellent relaxation tapes available.)

1   Find a time and a place where you will not be disturbed. Start by making yourself warm and comfortable, seated or lying down. Uncross your legs and rest your hands in your lap. If you prefer to listen to music, choose something slow and calming. Take your attention to your breath.

2   Fix your gaze on a spot across the room or on the ceiling. When your eyes start to tire, count five deep breaths backwards. With each breath, allow your eyes to close a little. When you get to one, close them.

3   Now take your attention to each group of muscles in turn and allow them to relax. Either start with your toes and feet, calves and ankles, thighs, etc and work up, or start with the top of your head and work down through the face, neck and shoulders, arms and hands and so on.

4   To deepen the relaxation, slowly count down from ten to one on each out breath. As you do so, imagine yourself descending a flight of steps. When you get to the bottom, imagine yourself in a comfortable relaxing place, such as a garden, a beach or a special sanctuary.

5   When you are deeply relaxed, think 'zero'. Then repeat the following affirmation slowly to yourself: 'I relax easily, quickly and deeply. Each time I relax, I go deeper and deeper. I am at peace.'

Using your intuitive powers

As your intuitive powers begin to develop, you will find you can tune in to them at any time. In addition, here are some purposeful ways of making full use of this new resource.

142

Sleeping on it: it helps to sleep on a decision before making your final preference. The subconscious is like a computer, able to sort through complex ideas without your conscious state interfering. It works for you 24 hours a day, including when you are asleep.

If you are struggling with a difficult decision, ask your intuition to help. As you're dozing off to sleep, focus on a problem or question, and ask your intuition to reveal the answer to you. Keep a pen and paper by your bedside so you can write down any answers immediately, otherwise you may not remember in the morning.

You will frequently wake up clear about what to do.

143

Problem solving: write down the problem and examine it carefully so that you fully understand it. Ask yourself, 'What's stopping me from solving the problem? How can I get rid of the blockages?' Deal with those if you can.

Next, write down all the solutions that you can think of. What seems to be the best solution? Try it out.

So far, you've mainly used your left brain. If this doesn't work, relax into the alpha state and ask your intuition to help. The answer may not come there and then, but sooner or later it will. Often it will pop into your head in the most unexpected moment. Expect a solution and keep your wits about you so you don't ignore it when it comes – intuitive answers often seem simpler and wiser than normal thinking.

144

Sitting for ideas: use this method whenever you need some inspiration. Take a half-formed idea and examine it closely. Think about it, research it, and formulate some key questions (intuition usually works best when you have gathered plenty of facts and sorted through the information). Have a notebook and pencil ready.

Sit patiently in a darkened room for an hour or so, asking for the answers to pop into your head. (Many brilliant insights and ideas simply popped into someone's head unexpectedly.) Jot down any ideas that come to you before you leave the room.

145

Ask a higher power for guidance: pretend you are asking for help from a higher power. (If you believe in a higher power you'll have no need to pretend.) Use a question and answer format. Ask a question on which you need advice, then listen carefully. Have a pen and paper ready and write down anything that comes to you. You can do this any time you need quick guidance or relief in stressful situations.

146

Mind mapping™ is a technique popularised by Tony Buzan (the mind map™ is a registered trade mark of the Buzan organisation). It is a graphical technique for generating and sifting through ideas. It reflects the way the brain works by utilising both left and right hemispheres.

Take a large piece of paper. Write the topic of interest in the centre and ask your mind for ideas. Each main theme is plotted like a branch spreading out from the centre. Each sub-theme is plotted like a minor branch. Eventually the page is filled with ideas (see example below).

Mind maps™ can be used for many purposes, including note taking, note making, revision and structuring ideas.

I used them to plan this book and structure each chapter. One of my initial mind maps is reproduced in the example.

To draw a mind map™:

1   Take a large piece of plain paper. Turn it on its side (landscape). Have to hand a set of coloured pens.

2 Write or draw your central idea (using pictures of diagrams is a good idea, since the right brain brings these into play) in the middle of the page.

3 Add the main branches using key words or images. Use colour. If you can draw a picture that represents an idea, do so.

4 Add more detail in the form of sub-branches, with more key words and images.

5 Make your mind map™ as pleasing to the eye as possible.

6 When you are sure you've exhausted every idea, use arrows to connect ideas that are linked in some way.

The example opposite shows the mind map™ I used (in black and white; the original was in colour) when initially planning the contents of this book. As you can see, the final result was slightly different from these first thoughts, but, as with most mind maps, it was a useful starting point.

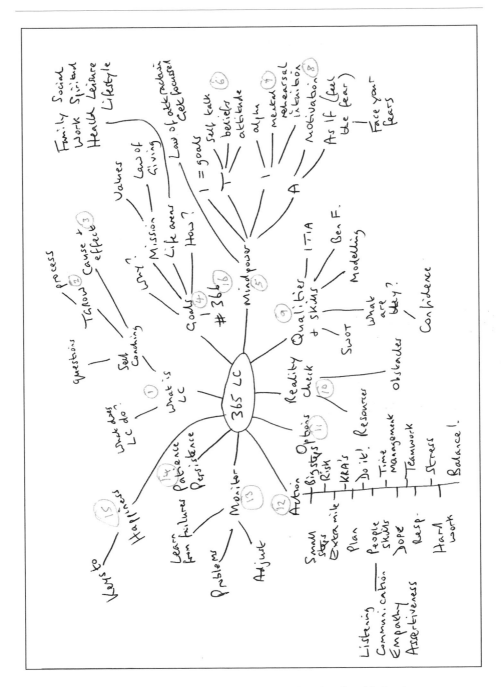

The mind map™ that started the planning for this book.

147

To heighten your intuitive and creative senses:

1   Notice what inspires and uplifts you and deliberately bring more of it into your life. For instance, if you like dancing, go dancing more; if you enjoy nature, go for a walk in natural surroundings regularly.

2   Seek out more inspiring situations.

3   Every day, do things that enthuse and stimulate you.

4   Spend more time around creative and inspirational people – it will rub off on you.

148

How to recognise your intuition: intuition works in subtle ways. Usually it reveals itself quietly. Sometimes it makes itself known in a dream. Many dreams are of little consequence – they are simply your subconscious cleaning out the mental cobwebs while you sleep – but a memorable or recurring dream may be a sign that your intuition is trying to get through to you.

The best way to recognise your intuition is to ask yourself, 'Does this feel right in my gut' (intuition is often called 'gut feel').

Also, take note of the first feeling or flash of thought. We initially experience something as a physical feeling a split second before we intellectualise about it. The first response is usually the most reliable because the left brain has not yet had time to come up with a conditioned response.

In general, the stronger the feeling of fulfilment and contentment, the more likely it is to be your intuition.

149

Trust your instincts. Intuitive perception is rarely wrong. You subconsciously gather all sorts of ideas and information which fuel your intuition. You won't even be aware of most of it – that's why we call it *sub*conscious. Talk to people who've made good decisions and they'll often tell you they don't really know why they did what they did, it just felt right.

Sometimes the rational mind suggests one thing and intuition the other. You're not sure which to follow. Find out what you need to know, make a decision, then ask your intuition if it is correct. If your deepest self turns against it, don't do it.

The more you tune in to your intuition and rely on it, the better it works for you.

Use your imagination

Imagination is more important than knowledge. It is a preview of life's coming attractions.

Albert Einstein

First dream your life, then live your dream

150

Everything that has ever been created by a human being originated as a mental image in someone's imagination. This was then made real through a combination of ingenuity, clear thinking and physical effort. We are what and where we are because we have first imagined it.

Time spent imagining your perfect future is never wasted, because anything your mind can envisage can be materialised. Choose to see yourself as a happy, successful, healthy and gifted person. When you think, imagine, talk and behave like the person you want to be, you will become that person. There is no obstruction other than a 'can't' way of thinking.

151

You may not always be aware of them, but you are continually making pictures in your mind. These pictures have a favourable effect if they are positive (and, in contrast, a harmful effect if they are negative). Napolean Hill recognised this in his groundbreaking book, *Think and Grow Rich*. He wrote, 'What the mind can conceive, the will can achieve.'

That's why top sportsmen and women use creative imagery and autosuggestion to help them win trophies and break world records; business executives use them to help make better sales presentations and gain promotion; leading doctors teach patients to relieve painful symptoms and even rid themselves of serious diseases, including cancer, arthritis and heart disease, using these techniques; and psychotherapists use them to help their clients overcome a wide range of emotional problems using them, including fears and phobias, panic attacks, eliminating unwanted habits, stress and lack of confidence.

Become aware of the pictures in your mind. Some of these will be fleeting, others more long-lasting.

152

Think about your ideal life. What does it look like, feel and sound like? Imagine the way you want to live, the people you want to mix with, your work, your home, the lifestyle you desire, your hobbies and interests and so on. Create a vision.

Don't worry at this stage about the details – just outline your ideal life so you can begin to acquire the habit of believing it's possible.

Make some notes in your Self-Coaching Journal. Do it right now. Remember, life's too short to fritter on activities that don't fulfil you and you don't enjoy.

153   Imagine yourself five years from now, having accomplished a major goal.

Ask yourself:

■ What does it look like?

■ How does it feel?

■ What will have had to happen to me to be there?

■ What will I have had to have done for me to be there?

■ What steps will I have to have completed?

Now slowly move back in time, three years from now, two years, one year, six months, three months, one month, reviewing each successive step until you come back to today.

Write down some thoughts about this exercise in your Self-Coaching Journal.

Creative imagery

Creative imagery is simply imagining things, e.g. 'seeing' them in your mind's eye, or 'hearing', 'smelling', 'tasting' or 'feeling' them in your imagination.

Creative imagery works because it has an immediate and powerful impact on the subconscious mind. The material in your subconscious mind is largely responsible for your habitual behaviour patterns, because it contains all your programming and conditioning. This is very beneficial if the material is positive, because once an idea takes root in the subconscious, it's extremely difficult to shift.

Daily creative imagery sessions can help eliminate bad habits, create new habits and strengthen motivation. This is so for three main reasons:

First, the subconscious goal-seeking mechanism (see page 31) is most easily influenced by images, symbols and feelings. Holding a mental image in your mind or feeding in a vivid emotional experience makes a deep and lasting impact. Your subconscious takes it as an instruction to 'make it so'.

Second, the subconscious does not have the ability to distinguish between stimuli received through the five senses (i.e. the external world), and those coming from your imagination. It accepts whatever the conscious mind thinks about as real. Have you ever woken up at night in a sweat after a bad dream? Or cried at the cinema? You knew the experience wasn't real (because your rational conscious mind told you so), but still you were affected emotionally because your subconscious responded as if it was. It processes them in exactly the same way and stores them in your memory as if they were equally real.

Imagine you are biting into your favourite food. Can you taste it? Is your mouth watering? It usually does, despite the fact that the food exists only in your imagination. And as far as your memory is concerned, you really did just enjoy a mouthful of your favourite food.

Third, the subconscious is housed in the right brain, which is the visual and emotional part of the brain. This is why 'a picture is worth a thousand words' – it reaches parts of the brain that language alone cannot reach.

Creative imagery works most effectively when your mind and body are deeply relaxed and in the alpha state. Entering the alpha state for even a few minutes a day is enormously beneficial. Coupled with autosuggestion, creative imagery is an effective technique for changing limiting beliefs and mental images because it bypasses the conditioned conscious mind and communicates your desires directly to the subconscious.

Getting the most from creative imagery

Just about any dream grows stronger if you hold on a little longer.

Margo Gina Hart

154

Before you use these techniques, make sure your intentions are clear.
Decide on the contents of each session in advance. Creative imagery is
powerful, but if unfocused can inadvertently do more harm than good.

If you have difficulty remembering your routine, record it onto a
cassette tape or write it down and ask a friend to read it to you slowly.

155

Make time every day – preferably twice a day. The best times are first
thing in the morning when, as you awaken, you are naturally in alpha,
and in those twilight moments just before you drop off to sleep. Your
last few thoughts and mental images of the day have a huge impact on
your subconscious and may influence your dreams.

156

Relax your body and calm the mind. Sit or lie quietly, close your eyes
and imagine you have a mental screen inside your forehead, just above
eye level. Use this to create the images you want. Let your mind wander
to relaxing feelings and images, but don't force it; this is a very passive
process. *Allow* your chosen images to materialise. Too much effort can
be self-defeating.

157

Use all five senses as much as possible. Create visual images and try to make any sounds, textures, smells and feelings as clear and distinct as you can.

If you have difficulty visualising, don't worry, you're not alone and you will improve with practise. Start by picking a scene you know well, perhaps your home or garden. Close your eyes and think of a small part of it – a tree, the front door or a window. Let an image materialise. If it doesn't, *pretend* you can see it. Then open your eyes, pause a few seconds, close them and try again. Can you see it?

Make your imagination come alive. Place the images in the middle of your mental screen, and use colour, brightness and movement.

158

Imagine the scene as you would experience it through your own senses, not as an onlooker. For example, if you want to be an actor, imagine yourself looking out at the audience from the stage. Smell the greasepaint, feel the boards beneath your feet, and hear the words projecting from your mouth just as you would as if you were speaking them.

159

Concentrate on yourself making a success of what you're doing. This is what you want to imprint on your subconscious.

For example, if your goal is to win the cup at the local tennis club, 'see' yourself holding the cup, milking the applause. Once they have registered in your subconscious, your habits (of thought and action) will automatically adjust themselves to bring your mental images into reality. Conjure up as much upbeat emotion as you can. The more feeling you put into it, the better.

160

Enhance your creative imagery with autosuggestion. Choose suitable suggestions, such as:

- Every day in every way I get closer and closer to achieving my goal.

- I only think about and visualise what I want to happen.

- I am worthy of all the good in my life. I deserve the best.

- I think, talk and act confidently at all times.

- I believe in myself. I can do anything I choose.

- I am successful in everything I do.

161

Practise. The more often you use creative imagery, the easier it gets. Use it daily even if you can only spare a few minutes. Frequent short sessions are better than long, irregular sessions.

Now take action. Creative imagery smoothes the way to success, providing you do what has to be done. But don't expect too much all at once. If nothing seems to happen for a while, don't give up. Lasting change takes time, patience and persistence.

162

Choose something you want for yourself and practise using creative imagery every day.

Start with something small. After a month, review your progress. What's changed? How close are you to your goal? Have you achieved it? How do you feel? How well has creative imagery worked for you? What more do you need to do?

163

The **manifestation technique** is a potent way of bringing together the power of intention, positive thinking, creative imagery and goal-directed action.

1   Start by drawing a line down the centre of a large sheet of paper. Head the left side 'Reasons why I want...' (a car, house, job, personal quality, loving relationship or whatever it may be).

2   Head the right side 'Specific details of my...'

3   Now list all the reasons why you want it in the left column; on the right side, opposite each reason, list precisely what you want. The more specific, the better.

Reasons why I want a ...	Specific details of my ...

For example, let's suppose you have set your heart on a new house:

Reasons why I want a new house	Specific details of my new house
Present house too big (family grown up and moved away).	Three good sized bedrooms, living room, dining room, study, downstairs toilet.
Garden too big – too much work.	Medium sized garden facing south, easy to maintain.
No garage, no off road parking.	Garage and off road parking.
Would like a patio and conservatory.	Patio and conservatory facing south.
Noisy neighbourhood.	Quiet neighbourhood in a convenient location.
Neighbours overlook current house	Not overlooked.
No downstairs toilet.	Downstairs toilet.
Affordable price.	Price range: £250,000–£300,000

4   You now have two detailed columns with your requirements on the right reflecting the reasons on the left. Read through it a few times until you are clear about what you want and the image is etched on your mind. Write down some pertinent affirmations on a small card to carry with you.

5   Now lie down or sit back, take a few deep breaths, close your eyes and relax. Imagine and affirm yourself with what you want, and feel deeply grateful for having the means to acquire it.

    For example, imagine your house as already yours. Picture it. 'See' yourself standing in the garden or sitting out on the patio. Smell the freshly mown lawn. Now turn the front door handle and enter your house. Imagine living there, feeling joyful. Feel grateful in advance for your goal being accomplished.

6   Now do what needs to be done. Obviously your desires will not materialise out of thin air, but if you reinforce the mental images daily and avoid allowing doubts to creep in, your subconscious autopilot will not forget. You will be guided by your intuition, and if you believe in yourself, your wishes will come true.

Try the manifestation technique for yourself. (I used it last year when I needed a small car, and was given – yes, *given* – a perfectly adequate one that met my requirements by a complete stranger at a seminar. Strange but true!)

---

164   **Mental rehearsal** is the practice of running a forthcoming event through in your mind in advance. It helps you do better on the day.

    It's simple. When you face an anxiety provoking situation, spend a few minutes each day leading up to the event to relax and make a clear image of yourself completely calm and in control. For example, say you had a driving test a fortnight from now. Every day for the next two weeks, mentally rehearse the test. 'See', 'feel' and 'hear' yourself going through the test, culminating in the examiner congratulating you and handing you your pass slip. If you did this daily, by the time the test arrived you would be confident and at ease, and much more likely to pass.

Dr Roger Bannister used mental rehearsal to prepare himself for his attempt on the four minute mile. When a journalist asked him how he felt as he rounded the final bend with the world record within reach, he said he'd felt perfectly calm. 'I'd done it so many times in my mind,' he said, 'I just had a feeling of *déjà vu*.'

Try it. Use mental rehearsal to prepare yourself for a forthcoming situation. Choose one you don't normally handle well. Go through the entire event in advance in your mind. See yourself going through every step exactly as you would like to do it in reality, affirming that you are successful and achieving your desired outcome. Once you've tasted the benefits, you'll want to use the technique often.

165

Anchoring: an 'anchor' is any stimulus that triggers an emotional response. It could be a piece of music that evokes happy or sad memories for you, a visit to a favourite place, or a photograph of someone who you care about. Anchoring provides a short cut to positive feelings at any time: your emotionally-charged memories become a powerful resource to help change your emotional state at will.

This is how: let's say you need to make a sales call and you're feeling nervous. Relax into alpha. Take your mind back to a time when you felt really confident. (If one doesn't come to mind, just pretend you feel confident – your subconscious mind won't know the difference.)

When the feeling is really strong, tighten your fist and say the words 'Yes! I can!' (Any suitable gesture or phrase is just as good, provided that it is not one you use habitually.) Then tell yourself that every time you do this you'll experience those same powerful feelings all over again. This is called **installing the anchor**.

Just before the sales call, tighten your fist and repeat the chosen phrase. This is called 'firing' the anchor. You'll feel all that confidence come flooding back. If you've never done it before, you'll be amazed how effective it is.

The more you rehearse your anchor, the more successful you will be. Also, make sure those empowering feelings are really intense when you install it, because if you are feeling indifferent you will not succeed. Also, an anchor which has not been used for some time will lose its power and fade away. If you don't use it, you may lose it!'

166

Install an anchor that you can use whenever you need confidence, and reinforce it several times a week. Choose any confident word, phrase or gesture that works for you.

Also install an anchor that you can use when you need to feel calm, and reinforce it several times a week. This time, choose a word, phrase or gesture that brings you peace and quiet composure.

167

The **swish technique** is another way of creating a powerful emotional state at will. It can be used to develop confidence, drive, enthusiasm, calmness, determination and so on. Let's suppose you wish to grow in confidence:

1   Think back to a time when you felt confident (there must be one – if not, imagine such a time). What stops you feeling like this normally?

2   Now think of a time when you felt unsure of yourself. What made you feel that way? Was it within yourself, or something another person said or did?

3   Break your concentration by looking at something around you or reciting your telephone number backwards.

4   Next create an image of yourself a few minutes into the future, as someone with confidence, poise and high self-esteem. Make this image as vivid as possible, and 'feel' it as the truth. Say an affirmation, such as 'I think, talk and act confidently at all times,' or, 'I believe in myself. I can do anything I choose.'

5   When the positive image is clear and firm, shrink it down to a glistening dot and put it in the middle of the negative image evoked. Let the dot grow until, with a loud 'swish' it blocks out and engulfs the negative image. Do this several times, letting the swish happen more and more quickly.

6   When you are ready, try to recall the negative image. The positive should have replaced it, and you will be experiencing a shimmering cloud of good feelings all around you. If not, go back to step 5 and practise some more.

168

Now that you have learned several creative imagery techniques, ask yourself:

■ What goal(s) could I achieve more quickly if I used creative imagery, mental rehearsal, anchoring and swish?

■ How can I improve my use of these techniques?

169

Overcoming problems with creative imagery.

If you diligently set aside time for creative imagery and autosuggestion and nothing seems to happen, ask yourself the following questions:

■ Do I really want this? Or am I fooling myself? (The more you want something, and the more you believe that it will be yours, the more likely you are to get it.)

■ Am I being too impatient? Have I allowed sufficient time?

■ Am I willing to do what needs to be done?

■ Am I trying too hard? Am I trying to force it?

■ Have I allowed doubts to creep in? (Doubt – especially self-doubt – takes you right back where you started.)

And remember: merely reading this book without applying what you learn won't accomplish anything at all.

The 'as if' principle

> *If one advances confidently in the direction of their dreams and endeavours to lead a life which they have imagined, they will meet with a success unexpected in common hours.*
>
> **Henry David Thoreau**

170

The fourth part of the ITIA formula for permanent change is **action**. The secret is to behave as if you are already the person you most want to be; then, like a professional actor, you become that person.

Shakespeare, who was no mean psychologist, expressed this principle in simple terms when he wrote, 'Assume a virtue if you have it not'. This is precisely what many successful people did when they first set out to tackle a challenging goal.

The 'as if' principle states that when you act 'as if' the changes you desire will happen and are already happening, they are inevitable. When you act as if success is inevitable, it invariably is. And if you behave in a confident way, whether you are feeling confident or not, people around you will believe in you, which will make it easier to believe in yourself, hence your confidence grows.

Many therapists use the 'as if' principle in their work with panic attack and phobia sufferers. They take clients with fear of heights to the top of tall buildings and encourage them to stay there until their anxiety subsides. They bring spiders progressively closer to arachnophobics until they are comfortable in their presence, and patients with social phobias are encouraged to mix with people in controlled settings until their panic diminishes.

These methods have been shown to help a considerable number of sufferers, and are even more effective when coupled with cognitive therapy (i.e. working with attitudes and beliefs) and creative imagery. There will be times as you progress towards your goals when a certain course of action seems too daunting and mental rehearsal alone is insufficient to take away the apprehension. At these times, you must simply grit your teeth, feel the fear and do it anyway. Change never feels right, but when you act 'as if', eventually the uncomfortable feelings die away.

171

Think of a personal attribute you would like to develop, such as assertiveness, patience, confidence, calmness or courage. Find out what people who have this trait do, and behave that way for a week. For example, if you are shy find out how outgoing people behave and do likewise. Make a special effort to shake hands firmly, look people in the eye, speak with a self-assured tone of voice and smile. Sooner or later your initial distress will diminish.

A touch of anxiety is part of the growth process. Consider the butterflies in your stomach to be nothing more than growing pains. Anxiety does not increase for ever, eventually it fades. (It fades much more quickly when backed up with a change of thinking and use of creative imagery.) Then the new behaviour becomes a natural part of you, and the very same mechanisms that once tried to prevent you from changing throw their weight behind the new way of being.

Motivating yourself

Motivation is an inner drive that compels you to action. Motivation is vital if you want to change or achieve anything. Motivated people have more enthusiasm, more energy, persistence, resilience and creativity.

Some people appear more driven to succeed than others. Why? Is it just something one is born with – or can you increase your level of motivation and use it to move yourself towards a better future? The answer is yes. How? By gaining a better understanding of motivation and *applying* the tools and techniques you're learning about.

172

Early experiments on animals concluded that we are motivated simply by a 'felt need'. For example, place a starving rat and a piece of cheese in a maze and it searches for the food. Repeat this daily, and the time taken to find the cheese diminishes until after a few days it will go straight through the maze to the cheese. The rat is motivated by a felt need, i.e. it is hungry, which induces stress, and its goal (the cheese).

Think about it – what, in life, is the 'cheese' for you?

173

Once a need or want is experienced, we face certain decisions. What is the best way of alleviating that need? How much effort would it take? Is it worth the effort? This leads us to the second point about motivation: the way we go about meeting a felt need depends on the amount of anticipated 'pleasure' or 'pain' that will result from any given action.

To return to the rat briefly, it knew from experience that eating relieves tension and is pleasurable, and that not eating causes discomfort (pain). Therefore, when hungry it is motivated to search for food. Once it has eaten, it is content to go back to sleep.

Look again at your list of goals. Differentiate between your *real* needs and wants, and *superficial* wants. Superficial wants don't come from your inner self, and consequently don't motivate.

Also remember – only an *un*satisfied need motivates.

174

We humans continually weigh up the choices available to us and choose those which appear to offer the most pleasure and cause the least pain. For example, if you were relaxing on a sunny beach after a good lunch, with no pressing engagements, you would probably be happy to stay for the whole afternoon. But, as mealtime approaches, you begin to feel restless until, like the rat, you head off in search of food.

Some people are more motivated by the desire to avoid pain (physical, mental or emotional) than to seek pleasure. Their principal style is 'moving away' motivation. Pain avoiders recall previously undesirable situations and try to avoid them happening again. They prefer to stay in their 'comfort zones' rather than risk striving for new challenges.

Sometimes it's more a matter of avoidance tactics, for instance, teenagers who put off studying avoid the immediate 'displeasure' of work in order to enjoy the short term 'pleasure' of watching TV. Then as their exams approach, the prospect of failing looms large, so they choose the path which offers the least long-term pain and get stuck in.

The reverse is true for high achievers – they are nearly always attracted by the prospect of more 'pleasure', so they are willing to risk a little extra 'pain'. Every time they succeed in finding their 'cheese', this behaviour is reinforced. Pleasure seekers focus on good experiences and try to hang on to them. This is 'moving towards' motivation.

Are you (by nature) a 'pleasure seeker' or 'risk avoider'?

175

Research shows that the most powerful motivation comes from a combination of passion and purpose. These are derived from:

1   A detailed and vivid image of what you want.

2   Strong desire.

3   A firm belief that you will be successful.

This is why clear goals, creative imagery (see pages 101–105) and positive beliefs and expectations are so important.

176

Moving away motivation. William was brought up in a deprived industrial area during the Great Depression of the 1920s and 30s. In his youth, tired and hungry after a 12 hour shift in a hot and steamy soap factory, he dragged his aching body to evening classes to gain additional qualifications before returning to the small family home with no bathroom and an outside toilet where he shared a bedroom with two brothers.

'I couldn't stand the prospect of spending the rest of my life in a factory,' he said, 'and I didn't want my family to suffer as I had.' He retired a prosperous man, living in a comfortable home in a leafy suburb.

Body Shop founder Anita Roddick was primarily concerned with rectifying a disagreeable situation – cruel animal experiments – when she started making her own cosmetics. Now, the Body Shop is an international business bringing joy to people around the world and Anita is a very wealthy woman. But it is still driven by the desire to fight cruelty to animals, promote justice and protect the environment.

Both William and Anita were driven by 'moving away' motivation. How about you?

177

Extrinsic motivation comes from outside. There are two main types:

- Fear motivation, e.g. a sergeant major in the army bullies and harasses new recruits to knock them into shape. Fear motivation is effective in the short term, but is short-lived.

- Incentive motivation, e.g. an employer offering a bonus for good performance, or a child receiving sweets for good behaviour. This is effective for a while but, like a drug, the amount and frequency of the incentive usually needs to be increased over time if motivation is to be maintained. Also, motivation can fade away if the incentive is withdrawn.

To what extent are you motivated by fear, incentives, or both?

178

Intrinsic motivation comes from within. It is impervious to the words and actions of others, therefore it is the most powerful type. Clear goals that come from within, a detailed and vivid image of what you want, strong desire and self-belief are the bases of strong intrinsic motivation. Without these you're unlikely to have enough motivation to keep going when the going gets tough.

" *Nothing constructive and worthy of man's efforts ever has or ever will be achieved except by that which comes from a positive mental attitude, based on a definiteness of purpose and activated by a burning desire, and acted upon until the burning desire is elevated to the level of applied faith.*

Dr Napolean Hill "

Staying motivated

The key to staying motivated lies in our old friend, the ITIA formula.

179

Intention: keep your goals very clearly etched in your mind. Remind yourself daily of your aims and commitment. Encourage yourself by keeping a physical symbol of your goals in sight. If it's a material object you're after, carry a photograph with you, if a personal development goal, something that symbolises its achievement.

Don't rest on your laurels. Once you've achieved a goal – set some more. Keep the momentum going. Without goals you lose your drive, direction and inspiration.

180

Thought: the more positive your thinking, the more likely you are to succeed. Affirm daily, aloud, that you can and will achieve your goals. Challenge any disempowering beliefs. Be careful to ask yourself only purposeful questions.

181

Imagination: imprint your desires – and the belief that they will come true – on your subconscious mind daily. Every morning and evening – and at frequent intervals in between – imagine yourself in clear detail accomplishing your goals, and use mental rehearsal, anchoring and swish when appropriate.

182

Do something every day towards your goals. Not only does this take you closer to them, but also helps to keep them in mind. Keep a 'to do' list and update it continually (see pages 160–162 on time management). Monitor your progress and make adjustments if necessary and, above all, keep going.

If it feels awkward, ignore the discomfort, feel the fear and do it anyway. Change never feels right, but when you act 'as if', over time the unpleasant feelings grow fainter and die away.

183

Celebrate your progress. Each time you reach a major stepping stone, give yourself a pat on the back. Treat yourself to something special – a lavish meal, an outing to somewhere special, a massage, sauna, whatever you fancy. Having something to look forward to when you reach a significant milestone is very motivating. Record your thoughts in your Self-Coaching Journal.

If things don't work out as planned, reflect on what you've learned and put it all down to experience. Whatever you do, don't castigate yourself. Instead, reaffirm your commitment and keep going.

184

If you've tried your hardest and you still find it hard to stay motivated, it may be that the goal(s) you are chasing is not right for you. You may, for instance, have drawn the wrong conclusions, listened to the wrong people, or misinterpreted your intuition. If you suspect this may be the case, re-examine your goals. Go back to the section on discovering your purpose (pages 34–36) and work through the process again.

Step two: summing up

As a human being your ability to reflect on your experiences and think and act for yourself is your greatest asset. Your success in any walk of life ultimately depends on what you think, say, imagine and do. These are the major **causes** – your life itself and how you feel about it are the **effects**, and since you're in charge of your thoughts, word, imagination and actions, you're in charge of your destiny too.

Negative thinking is probably the main single reason why many people do not achieve their goals. It is a habit, usually learned in childhood; it has nothing whatsoever to do with your genes. Unwanted thinking patterns can be changed with just a little willpower and patience.

The ITIA formula is a complete approach to positive mental conditioning. Fix your intentions (goals); correct negative self-talk and dispute unhelpful beliefs; constantly affirm and envision your happiness and success; and identify the actions that will take you closer to your goals and keep doing them.

Step three: building desirable personal qualities into yourself

4

If your dreams and ambitions still seem a long way off, it could be because you have not yet developed the core personal qualities you need. Obviously these qualities vary according to your individual proclivities and chosen field, but some are common to all. Some, like patience, determination, concentration, people skills, enthusiasm and a sense of humour never go amiss whatever your goals.

The personal attributes you bring to your activities are the most valuable resources you have. But can we change? I frequently hear comments like, 'I'm a ditherer – that's just the way I am.' If you believe that's just the way you are, you may find the whole idea of letting go of unwanted traits and developing new ones a little daunting. Let's take a closer look at what's possible and what is not.

We are born with about one-third of our character traits already in place through our genes and biochemistry. These play a part in shaping certain aptitudes and talents. They also influence our level of introversion or extraversion, placidity or volatility, and tendency to certain conditions such as depression and compulsive behaviours. Our physical make up is also predetermined to some degree.

Obviously, without the right physical make up you will never make it as a supermodel, win a gold medal at the Olympics, or sing like Placido Domingo. If you have little talent, effort alone will not enable you to write songs like Lennon and McCartney, act like Gwynneth Paltrow or paint like Salvador Dali. I'm not suggesting for a moment that these people didn't have to work hard to develop their talents – they certainly did. But without their innate natural abilities they would not have reached such heights.

So what of the remaining two-thirds of our character? This is a result of our environment and conditioning, our learning, and, even more importantly, our way of thinking. Some attitudes are deeply ingrained, but can still be modified. Remember, anything which has been learned can be unlearned and relearned.

You won't succeed at your major goals unless you acquire the qualities, knowledge and skills you need. When you start on a goal, you may not have all the personal attributes required; nevertheless, if the goal is right for you, you can develop them, provided you are willing and determined.

Who do you think you are (and who would you like to be)?

185

Who do you think you are? In your Self-Coaching Journal, write two or three sentences that summarise your most important personal attributes. Don't think too hard – just write whatever comes into your mind.

186

In the chart opposite, write down ten qualities you most admire in other people in the left-hand column. Think about your family, work colleagues and friends. Think about people you've read about or seen in films or on TV. Also think about *fictional* characters from TV or film. What is it about them that you admire?

Then in the other column write down ten personal qualities you would like for yourself.

If you can think of more than ten – fine – list these at the bottom of the page or on a separate sheet.

Personal qualities I most admire in others	Personal qualities I want for myself
1	
2	
3	
4	
5	
6	
7	
8	
9	
10	

187 Write a few sentences on how your life would be different if you had all the qualities you listed in 186.

188

Now it's time to get to know yourself even better. You're going to carry out a personal **SWOT analysis – strengths**, **weaknesses**, **opportunities** and **threats**.

We are all weaker in some areas than others, but if it is important enough, we can work on our weaknesses and turn them into strengths. Knowing your strengths and weaknesses helps you to:

- Choose suitable goals.

- Know what you need to achieve these goals.

- Be realistic about which situations you handle well and where you need to improve.

- Make a plan to build on your strengths and eliminate or lessen your weaknesses.

Use the grid below. 189 to 192 will help.

My strengths (189)	My weaknesses (190)
Opportunities (191)	**Threats (192)**

189

Identify your strengths. You need to be aware of your personal strengths and reflect on how you could use them better.

- What are you good at?

- Where lies your greatest area of knowledge?

- What personal qualities do you have?

- What makes you unique?

- What wouldn't you want to change?

- How do you learn best. By doing? Reading? Formal study? Watching and copying? Taking part in discussions? Listening to audiotapes? Through mentoring or coaching?

Have you overlooked any? Don't be modest. Most people can think of at least a couple of dozen if they put their minds to it. Check that your modesty isn't preventing you boasting a bit, or the perfectionist in you isn't stopping you being satisfied with something that is very good but less than faultless.

(If you find this difficult, don't try to finish your list all at once; write down a few points every day. Don't worry if some appear trivial – you may have overlooked their importance.)

190

List your weaknesses:

- What do you consider to be your weaknesses?

- Where are the gaps in your knowledge?

- What qualities do you lack?

- What aspects of yourself do you find hard to accept?

- What would you want to change?

Don't go overboard listing weaknesses. It's good to be realistic, but not so good to exaggerate them. You need to be aware of weaknesses not so that you can dwell on them, but improve.

Beware of comparisons – the quickest way to deflate your spirits is to compare yourself with other people, especially the wrong people.

Some of the things you find hard to accept about yourself may be impossible to change. If you are 5'2" and would rather be 6'2", there is little you can do. Everyone has some aspect of themselves they wish were different. All you can do is refuse to allow it to interfere with your happiness and get on with your life.

But if change is possible, there's no point in complaining. Do something about it. If you don't make the effort, you'll stay exactly as you are and you've only got yourself to blame.

191

Identify the opportunities available to you. Your aim in identifying opportunities is to recognise areas you want to develop further, e.g. new personal attributes, qualifications, experiences, health and fitness, improved communication skills, etc.

Start by thinking about your strengths. For each strength write down how you could make better use of it in the future. Then consider:

■ What opportunities do you have right now?

■ What other opportunities could you create if you developed a particular strength or improved upon a weakness?

■ What have you overlooked?

192

Threats: What would be the consequences of staying as you are? Which of your goals would be most at risk? From where, what or from whom do the threats come?

193

If you're still not sure about your strengths and weaknesses, get some feedback from others. Choose people you know well, who know you and whom you trust – your partner, perhaps, or a best friend, work colleague or boss. Many people have an annual appraisal at work – if you did, what did you learn about yourself? Was it useful?

Ask these people to tell you what they think you're good at, what you do well, and what you're not so good at. Ask them what, in their opinion, you need to develop and what you could do to improve.

This may not be easy, so be patient, don't take offence and seek clarification if you don't understand. If they say something you disagree with, find out more about why they take this view. When they've finished, thank them.

In your Self-Coaching Journal write down:

■ What did you learn about yourself from this exercise?

■ What will you do differently as a result?

■ What was good about their feedback?

■ What was not so good about their feedback?

194

Imagine someone has asked you for a written personal reference for yourself. What would you write?

The qualities of success

Certain qualities and skills are common to most successful people. The main ones are in the sections below.

195

Self-belief is fundamental. Without it, you're likely to underachieve in every life area, and have problems in all your personal and professional relationships.

Ask yourself:

■ Do I believe deep down that I am worthy of the good things I can create for myself?

■ To what extent do I show faith in myself in the way I speak and behave?

■ How much do I like, respect and approve of myself?

196

Self-reliance: successful people know that the responsibility for making their lives work lies with them. Although they enjoy being and working with others, they also know that it's important to trust themselves and rely on their own judgement.

Those who are quick to blame bad luck when things go wrong are seldom happy and rarely accomplish very much.

■ Do you trust yourself?

■ When was the last time you made a major decision using your own judgement in the face of opposition from others?

■ Do you feel you need other people's approval?

■ Do you feel free to make your own decisions, which truly reflect what you want out of life? If not, why not?

197

Commitment: committed people are motivated and disciplined in their approach. They are able to put aside all doubts and fears, and get on with the task in hand. Without commitment we are tempted to make excuses and look for an escape route when problems arise, rather than rolling up our sleeves and looking for a solution.

Look at your current list of goals. What is your level of commitment to each goal? Write a number between zero and ten next to each, where ten means you are totally and irrevocably committed, and zero means no commitment at all. Be completely honest with yourself. If you awarded less than, say, five, it's probably not a genuine goal at all; six – eight, and it may be worth rephrasing your goal; nine or ten, go for it!

198

Vision: successful people tend to have a clear vision or purpose. They are forward looking. They create a wonderful life for themselves in their imagination. They're inspired because they have so much to look forward to.

Do you have a vision of how you want your life to be? If so:

■ Is it clear?

■ Does it feel real?

■ Does it excite you?

■ What could you do to clarify your vision and make it even more real?

199

Self-control: the power for our lasting success and happiness lies in being able to do what needs to be done when we need to do it, and in avoiding what would not be advantageous. This takes discipline and self-control. We don't always feel like doing those essential but unpleasant tasks.

Self-control is not necessarily synonymous with pain and suffering; just concentrating on what's important until the job is done. Doing what we love doesn't mean we won't occasionally have to make short-term sacrifices, but when we feel good about our goals disciplined effort doesn't feel that bad.

Ask yourself:

■ Do I always complete what I begin?

■ Do I have any bad habits I can't seem to break?

200

Concentration is focusing your mind on what you're doing and what needs to be done.

When we concentrate any form of energy, including mental energy, it intensifies. Place a piece of wood in the hot sun, and nothing much would happen; but, as any schoolboy knows, focus the sun's rays through a magnifying glass and it bursts into flames. Never underestimate the power and potency of concentrated mindpower.

Concentration needs to be worked on and developed. Over the past 20 years the average attention span of adults has halved. In most young people it is less than ten minutes.

201

Exercise to improve concentration. How good is your concentration? If not good enough, do this exercise every day.

■ Sit in a chair, back straight, feet flat on the ground, hands in your lap. Keep your body still.

■ Close your eyes, take a couple of deep breaths and allow yourself to relax more deeply with each breath. Allow your mind to settle.

■ Concentrate on one thing. Place a single image on your mental screen – a flower, a candle, a circle, anything that comes easily. Focus on that single image.

■ Whenever you find a stray thought entering your mind, stop it. Think only of the image on which you're concentrating.

After a fortnight, reflect on your progress. Has this exercise got easier? Has your concentration improved?

202

Knowledge: there are three types of knowledge:

1   Knowledge that is useful or essential to achieving your goals. This kind of knowledge is in itself priceless, providing it is applied. Seek it, use it, develop it, cherish it.

2   Knowledge that is pleasurable and fun to acquire, for example the sort that features in crosswords, quiz shows and general knowledge games. Welcome it, enjoy it.

3   Knowledge that is useless, misleading or destructive. Train yourself to recognise it, and avoid it.

What additional knowledge do you need in order to achieve your goals? Where could you find this information? In a library? DVD? Internet? From a friend or colleague? Do you need to go to college or take a self-study course? Would you consider going back into full-time education?

203

Enthusiasm: one of the most identifiable qualities of a total winner is an overall attitude of optimism and enthusiasm. This comes partly from having the right goals, but also from a general feeling of self-esteem and a conviction that life is to be enjoyed. Enthusiasm is infectious – to yourself and other people.

■   Are you enthusiastic about life generally?

■   Are you enthusiastic about achieving your goals?

> *Everyone is enthusiastic at times. One person has enthusiasm for 30 minutes, another for 30 days, but it is the one who has it for 30 years who makes a success in life.*
>
> **Edward B. Butler**

204

Initiative means making things happen rather than waiting for someone else to make a move (they usually don't!).

Successful people are enterprising and resourceful. They're willing to do whatever it takes. They're not afraid to grasp the nettle. And they know the difference between what is and what is not up to them.

Many years ago I was attending an open air event in Somerset, when I noticed that the wooden plank which served as a footbridge over the narrow stream between the camping field and the toilet block was broken. I reported it to one of the organisers. 'Well fix it,' he replied. 'Take the initiative. That's what this gathering is all about.'

Sometimes it is best to let events take their course. You must know when to hustle, and when to be patient, and this can be a difficult judgement to make. Once in a while if we ignore a problem, it goes away – but only once in a while. Usually it gets worse.

■ How good are you at taking the initiative?

■ Are you a self-starter?

■ What could you do to improve?

Once upon a time there were four people named Everybody, Somebody, Nobody and Anybody.
When there was an important job to be done, Everybody was sure Somebody would do it. Anybody could have done it, but Nobody did. When Nobody did it, Everybody got angry because it was Somebody's job. Everybody thought Anybody could do it but Somebody realised that Nobody would do it. So it ended up that Everybody blamed Somebody then Nobody did what Anybody could have done in the first place.

Anon.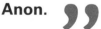

205

Integrity is having the courage to stick to your highest principles. Everyone wants to mix with people who are loyal, honest, reliable and keep their promises. When we do, we attract others of like mind. The confidence to act in accordance with your values and avoid engaging in anything you can't justify morally engenders a deep sense of self-respect and peace of mind.

Be honest with other people. Be honest with yourself. Then there's no need to play mind games, cover your tracks or struggle to remember what you said, when and to whom.

- Do you stick to your principles?

- Are your words matched by your deeds?

- Do others regard you as loyal, honest, reliable, trustworthy, dependable?

- Are you always honest with yourself?

- Do you ever feel the need to play mind games?

206

People skills: we all need friends and we all need to get on with others. You need people skills in the work area, and slightly different skills to be a friend, parent or lover. In business you need to know how to manage and motivate others, negotiate, persuade and, from time to time, give and receive criticism. In your personal relationships warmth, politeness, respect and genuineness never go amiss.

It's almost impossible to envisage how a person lacking people skills could succeed in this highly interdependent world. Think about it: if the product or service were the same, who would you rather buy from, someone who is warm and friendly, or cold and aloof? Would you rather have your hair cut by someone who makes pleasant conversation and treats you like an individual, or one who just gets on with the job without so much as a smile? And which of the two would you want as a friend?

We'll take an in-depth look at people and communication skills from page 188.

207

A sense of humour, fun and adventure. As every child knows (and adults all too easily forget), there's no point in doing anything you don't enjoy. Those who are full of the joys of living enjoy exploring and discovering new things. They radiate enthusiasm and have a keen sense of humour. Laughter is healthy and, as long as it is not cruel or destructive, healing.

- Do you have fun and adventure in your daily activities?

- What could you do to make them more enjoyable?

- How is your sense of humour?

Three ways to build new qualities into yourself (or reinforce existing ones)

If you recognise you need to acquire or strengthen certain personal qualities, here are three ways to speed your progress – our old friend the **ITIA formula**, **modelling** and the **Ben Franklin method**.

208

The ITIA formula:

1   Decide which qualities you wish to acquire. Write them down in the form of goals. Commit yourself to working on them. (Note: it may not be possible to set a firm deadline, since progress towards these goals is usually continuous and ongoing.)

2   Change your way of thinking. Amend your self-talk, veto negative thoughts, choose and use positive affirmations, challenge redundant beliefs, ask great questions and keep going.

3   Relax and imagine what it is like to already have your new qualities. What does it feel like? How is your behaviour different?

    Here is a simple routine for building confidence. It can easily be adapted for other attributes too.

- First, relax your body and mind, then 'see', 'hear' and 'feel' yourself as a confident and self-assured person.

- Next, 'visualise' yourself behaving confidently, relating to others with assurance.
- Then 'visualise' other people responding to you now that you are a confident person.

4   Act as if you already have the new qualities. Don't allow any uncomfortable feelings to get in the way.

209

Modelling: one way to acquire personal qualities is to use the modelling technique, a most effective learning tool.

From an early age, we adopt role models. Initially these are parents and relatives, but later include teachers, peers and media figures. We learned much of our early behaviour, including speech, by imitation.

Modelling is finding out how a successful person does something, then adopting their approach. It's one of the keys to accelerated learning. If you do what successful people do and become the kind of people they are, then you too will inevitably become successful.

To model effectively you must go beyond merely listening, watching and imitating another's behaviour and speaking habits. You must find out how they think and adapt their *attitudes* and *beliefs* to suit your own needs. But bear in mind, you will never copy someone else exactly, nor should you want to. You have your own special talents which add a special flavour to your experiences and activities.

Consider: who would you most like to model? Why? What is it about this person that you admire?

210

Is there something you would like to try but are afraid to? Then seek out someone who is currently doing it well. Listen and watch; find out all you can about the activity and what is required to do it well. Ask yourself, 'What would I have to believe in order to behave the same way?' Mentally 'see' yourself in their place.

Then do it.

211

The Ben Franklin method: Benjamin Franklin was a scientist, inventor, philosopher and philanthropist. He was a leading player in the American Revolution and one of the signatories of the Declaration of Independence.

As a young man he realised he would need to grow as a person if he were to achieve all his goals, so he made a list of 13 qualities he felt he needed to build into himself. He then worked on one a week. He reflected on what he would need to do to demonstrate that quality, then practised it for seven days. Then he moved on to the next and worked on that for a week.

After 13 weeks he went back to the top of his list, so at the end of the year he'd completed the cycle four times. When he felt he'd mastered a particular quality, he replaced it with a new one.

Benjamin Franklin was, in effect, using the ITIA formula, although understanding of the mind was fairly rudimentary in those days and he wouldn't have known it as such. The important thing is, it worked.

212

Cast your mind back to your SWOT analysis (188) and the feedback you received from friends and colleagues (193). Think about the personal qualities you most admire in others (186) and the person you would most like to model (209). Use these as the basis of making a definitive list of qualities you would like to acquire. Try to identify about a dozen.

Using the ITIA formula, work on one each week: set yourself a short-term goal, focus your mind on it, use creative imagery and practise whenever you have an opportunity.

When you reach the bottom of your list, take a fresh look at it, revise it if you wish, then start again.

Record your experiences in your Self-Coaching Journal. After a year, review your progress. What went well? What didn't? What further changes do you need to make in the coming 12 months?

Step three: summing up

Research shows that certain character traits are closely associated with happiness and success, and all of these particular traits can be nurtured, developed and strengthened. We are born with only about one-third of our character traits in place, which means the other two-thirds can be amended or acquired with patience, practice and determination.

Furthermore, we are born with no skills whatsoever – and no knowledge. All this is acquired as we continue to gain experience throughout our lives.

You can literally decide who you want to be and become that person. You now have the tools – go for it!

 # Step four: evaluating your current situation

Once your goals, your mental preparation and personal growth are under way, before going ahead with any far-reaching action take stock of your present situation. Try to understand all the factors which are impacting on your goal.

213

Where are you now in relation to your goal(s)?

- What actions have you taken so far?

- Did they get the right results? If not, why do you think that is?

- What's been holding you back?

- What stopped you going further?

- How much control do you have over these factors?

- What can you do to gain more control?

- When will you start?

Take time to reflect and make notes in your Self-Coaching Journal.

214

How do these factors impact on your goal(s):

- Physical resources.

- Financial resources.

- The economic climate.

- Your family and friends.

- Other people.

- Your knowledge and skills (or lack of them).

- Competitors.

- Publicity.

- Etc.

How do they affect your situation and your plans?

A man attended one of my life coaching courses recently. In the third week we were considering the qualities and skills each student felt they needed to achieve their major goals.

'I wish I had gone to college,' he sighed, 'then I would have the qualifications I need.'

'So why don't you go?' asked a fellow student.

'Because I'm 32 years old, and married with three children, and it would take me five years studying part-time in the evenings.'

'Tell me,' I asked him, 'how old will you be in five years if you go?'

'Thirty-seven,' he sighed.

'And how old will you be in five years if you don't go?'

He thought for a moment. '37, I suppose,' looking astonished that the age came out the same.

Next time you say to yourself, 'I can't do that because I'm too old,' ask yourself, 'How old will I be if I don't do it?' Then do it.

215

Starting a business? If you are thinking of starting your own business or already have one, think carefully.

- How far down that road are you?

- What is the nature of your product or service?

- What market are you in?

- Who are your customers or target customers? What do they buy now?

- Why should they buy from you in particular?

- Who are your competitors? How do/will you compete against them?

- How will market trends affect your business?

- How will you cope if your income is erratic?

216

What external resources do you need? External resources are those that lie outside yourself – finance, materials, equipment, fixtures and fittings, publicity, people and reputation and so on.

- Make a list of the resources you need (don't forget co-workers – do you need a team to help you, whose individual talents complement each other?).

- Which of these do you already have?

- For those you don't yet have, where and by when could you acquire them?

217

What obstacles will you have to overcome? Look clearly at each goal. What are the main obstacles? How will you overcome them? Don't try to hide from the uncomfortable parts of achieving it. You need to be aware of possible pitfalls so you are ready to deal with them.

If you are in business, or thinking of starting up, among the main obstacles you'll face are your competitors. Your competitors are also an invaluable resource; if you are willing to learn, they'll point out all your weaknesses and show you how to improve. Your main focus, of course, should be on bettering your own efforts; be aware of your competitors, but recognise that excessive worrying about a competitor's capabilities can be demoralising.

■ What obstacles do you face?

■ How will you overcome them?

■ What could you do about them right now?

218

Do your homework. Nowadays you can't take anything for granted. Knowledge can become obsolete in a few years, maybe months, even minutes (such as share prices, interest rates, exchange rates, etc). New ideas and innovations appear all the time.

Keep yourself up to date with anything which relates to your chosen field, right down to the nuts and bolts. Look for detailed answers to your questions. Sometimes one small piece of information can make all the difference. There are many potential sources – brochures, magazines, videos, websites, etc and personal contacts. Use them all.

I once worked in the head office of a large retailer. The marketing director spent a week every year stocking shelves in one of the company's superstores, closely observing what was going on and talking to the customers. He understood the importance of being in touch with what was going on and keeping his feet firmly on the ground.

■ What do you need to know to make progress with your goals?

■ How will you find the information?

■ When do you intend to search for it?

Step four: summing up

There's a traditional story about a couple lost in the countyside who spot an old farmer leaning against a gate.

'Please could you help us,' says the man, pointing at a map, 'we're lost and we want to get to here.'

The farmer peruses the map for a moment, then replies, 'It's not hard to find, but if I were you, I wouldn't start from here.'

Maps are only useful once you know exactly where you want to get to and your starting point. Where are you now? What do you have? What do you need? What stands in your way?

Being realistic is not the same as being negative. Yes, you will face challenges as you head towards your goals, and some of these may appear daunting at first. But remember – the challenges don't get any bigger, but *you* do!

6 Step five: considering your options

I often hear people say 'I had no choice,' or 'what choice do I have?', but it's a fact of life that we have choices – always. Sometimes we don't think we have, because we're not aware of them, in which case we must dig a little deeper. Sometimes the best option is the most obvious, but occasionally something we hadn't previously thought of turns out to be best.

219

Take each of your goals and ask yourself, 'What options do I have for achieving this goal?' Have a one person brainstorm and make a list. Ask around. Rule nothing out at this stage, no matter how far fetched it seems.

When you've exhausted your thoughts, look at each in turn. Examine them critically. Identify those that seem best.

Systematically look back over your options from time to time; reviewing them may spark off new ideas.

220

Screen out the least likely options and select the most likely. Consider *how* each of these could get the desired result and how *likely* it is to get the desired result. Think about the risks associated with each option.

If necessary make another shortlist, and check your level of commitment to pursuing each option and making it happen. Write a number between zero and ten next to each, where ten means you are totally committed, and zero means no commitment at all. Did you give one option a higher score than the others? Then go for it!

Step five: summing up

There's an unwritten law in self-coaching – you always have more options than you think you do. Some of these may turn out to be non-starters, others exactly the solution you were looking for.

Start by brainstorming. Ask yourself a constructive question. Write down everything that comes to you without analyzing or criticising. (The part of the mind that analyses and criticises is also the most heavily programmed and conditioned, which means it is the least likely to appreciate a creative, new idea.) Then, and only then, eliminate the non-runners and refine your list to say, the three or four most likely to succeed.

7 Step six: action – what you must do to succeed

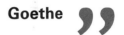

> *Whatever you can do, or dream you can, begin it.*
> *Boldness has genius, power and magic in it.*
> *Begin it now.*
>
> **Goethe**

The more active your orientation, the more you'll get done and the more you'll accomplish. In self-coaching, there are three types of action:

1   Those that take you closer to your goals. Obviously, your aim is only to identify and choose these actions. Do more of them, more intensively, and more often.

2   Those that have no effect either way. Some of these will be relaxing and pleasurable, so do them often; otherwise, avoid them. You have better things to do with your time.

3   Those that takes you further away from your goals. Steer clear of these as much as possible.

There is, of course, another alternative – do nothing – but this is not an option for anyone intent on getting more out of life. There's no point thinking great thoughts and imagining great accomplishments if you sit around and wait for something to happen. It won't. You must make it happen. Without taking action, you are like an aeroplane glued to the runway – full of potential but unable to fly.

Life coaches know that certain ways of doing things get results, so they encourage their clients to do those things. As a self-coach you can find out what they are for yourself.

221

Take responsibility. The starting point of all success is accepting full responsibility for yourself and the results you get. There's no such thing as luck, other than the luck you create for yourself by setting your own goals and working hard to achieve them.

In practice this means that from now on there are no more excuses and no blaming others when things don't go right.

- Do you accept full responsibility for your life and your behaviour?

- If not, why not? What changes in attitude and behaviour do you need to make?

The Law of Giving

 The man who will use his skill and constructive imagination to see how much he can give for a dollar, instead of how little he can give for a dollar, is bound to succeed.

Henry Ford

222

The Law of Giving affirms, in simple terms, that we receive through giving. When we do something for others, not only do we feel a sense of satisfaction, but we also contribute to the flow of prosperity. It's almost impossible to be happy and prosperous without being of service to others.

- In a commercial sense this means providing goods and services at the quality people want, when they want them and at a price they are willing to pay.

- In your personal, social and family life, it's offering friendship and showing consideration for others; a smile, a kind word and a few moments of your time are all precious gifts.

■ If your aim is to improve your performance in, say, sport, the performing arts or a hobby, it's about how much effort you are willing to make.

Giving is not just an action; it is also an attitude. If you give through gritted teeth or merely because you hope to get something back in return, you're unlikely to feel good and it probably won't work anyway since others will sense your true motives.

Everyone has plenty to give. We all have talents and skills which we can share, and when we find what we love and put our hearts and souls into it, our natural abilities develop naturally.

What do you have to give?

223

True success comes from helping people to help themselves. That's why the best life coaches make a good living – the more they help others, the more they thrive. When you include the welfare of others in your plans for success, you have a realistic chance of being successful. Thinking only of yourself usually spells disaster.

Think:

■ What do you give?

■ What could you give, that you don't at present?

■ To whom could you be of service?

■ How could you give more?

Write down some of the many ways that you can contribute to the happiness and wellbeing of people around you, in your community and your global family.

224

Get focused. Keep your goals very clearly etched in your mind.

■ Write your main goals on a small card and keep it with you in your wallet or purse.

■ Read through your list of goals and the benefits they will bring daily.

■ Frequently affirm that you can and will succeed and are on your way; also use autosuggestion.

■ At least once a day visualise yourself (in clear detail) accomplishing your goal.

■ Encourage yourself by keeping a physical symbol of your goal in sight, e.g. if you're working towards success in an exam or driving test, design a pretend certificate and hang it on your wall.

225

Make a plan. Once you've decided where you want to go the next challenge is working out how you'll get there. This is where planning comes in.

'The marvellous thing about lack of planning,' according to educationalist Peter Green, 'is that failure comes as a complete and utter surprise, and better still is not preceded by periods of stress and anxiety.' This aphorism highlights the habit of successful people of making plans, putting them into practice, and seeing them through. They know how to think ahead, set priorities, manage their time effectively and get things done.

Set clear and realistic deadlines and plot them on your wall chart or calendar, or in your diary. Nothing can galvanise you into action quite like a looming deadline.

Try to allow for every likely contingency. If your initial ideas turn out to be impractical, you can always think again.

Put your plans in writing. Have a plan of action for each of your main goals and read through it every week to check that you're on schedule. If there are unforeseen problems you can always make adjustments. Nothing is written in stone.

226

Get started. There is an ancient Chinese saying, usually attributed to Lao Tzu, 'Even the longest journey begins with a single step.' Take that first step now, even if you're not yet 100 per cent certain of all that needs to be done. Go on, ask for what you want. Make that tricky phone call. Just be aware that whenever you enter unfamiliar territory you are likely to experience at least some anxiety.

Once you've made a start, everything seems easier. It's like trying to push a broken-down car to the side of the road. It takes a mighty push to get it moving, but once the initial resistance is overcome there's no need to push quite so hard.

What can *you* do NOW to get started on your major goals?

227

Take massive action. There are times when you must concentrate all your energy and passion on a specific project without distraction, even if it means putting other activities to one side. These include:

■ When you first start.

■ When an important deadline is approaching.

■ When a particularly difficult task must be completed.

■ A final burst as you approach the winning tape.

Continually ask yourself:

■ How serious am I about achieving this goal?

■ Do my actions suggest real commitment?

■ If I were one of the most dynamic people in the world, what would I be doing? What actions would I be taking?

228

Hard work. You will never succeed at anything worthwhile unless you are willing to make the effort. Successful people work hard – harder than the average person – and they work smart. They believe in the old adage, 'The harder I work, the luckier I get.'

The prospect of hard work is off-putting for some, but it shouldn't be. When you find what you love doing, set goals, put your heart and soul into them, and make sure they benefit others as well as yourself, it doesn't feel like hard work.

" *To find a career to which you are adapted by nature, and then to work hard at it, is about as near to a formula for success and happiness as the world provides. One of the fortunate aspects of this formula is that, granted the right career has been found, the hard work takes care of itself. Then hard work is not hard at all.*

Mark Sullivan "

229

Get out of your comfort zone. Your comfort zone is that space (mental, physical or emotional) within which you feel relatively comfortable. Inside your comfort zone you do just alright, but once you move outside it anxiety takes over. In extreme cases this can bring on the fight or flight syndrome and cause sweating, palpitations, a dry throat, memory or concentration loss and so on – or sheer panic.

However, as you push at the boundaries of your comfort zone you find it expands. You become more at ease in situations which could previously have induced panic. And it's important that you should. Settling for what you have requires no risk, no change and no growth. That's OK if you are 100 per cent content with every aspect of your life – and if you are, that's wonderful; but life's greatest rewards are only available to those who go out on a limb once in a while. This doesn't mean being foolhardy, more a case of weighing up the odds and, if there's a fair chance of success, having a go.

I had an uncle who decided to quit a steady (but unexciting) job and relocate his family to an island off the Welsh coast. At that time English people were widely thought to be unwelcome in that part of Wales. Most of his friends thought he was mad, but he ignored their warnings. Five years later he had refurbished a beautiful old cottage in an idyllic seaside location, built a successful business and won round the locals. The critics had to admit he'd created a wonderful life for himself and his family.

Nothing of any note has ever been achieved without someone taking a risk. Those who are quick to tell you it can't be done are usually those who are afraid to take a risk themselves, and have done very little with their own lives.

There are three good reasons to leave your comfort zone from time to time:

- It's only through stretching and testing yourself that you grow.

- It's the only way to avoid an unadventurous and boring life.

- You will have to leave it sometime, however hard you resist. Life itself is ever-changing. Nothing ever stays the same for long.

Expand your comfort zone. Forecast the results of your actions as best you can, and get the best advice from people who have a track record in your field of activity. There's a huge difference between acting courageously and being foolish. Responsible risk-takers do their homework, have confidence in their abilities and are willing to have a go in the face of uncertainty.

230

Identify your **key result** areas. Usually you only need to excel at a handful of activities (usually no more than three or four) to be a leader in your field. Small differences in knowledge and ability can make or break a mission. In horse racing, millions of pounds can be won or lost 'on the nose'; one mark separates failure from success in examinations; half a teaspoonful of salt can render a meal inedible; and in business the company that launches a new product a few days ahead of its rivals often corners the market.

Often, it's the little things that make all the difference. Know what these are and master them.

231

Do it now! If there's something you want to do but have been putting off, do it now. If you keep putting off till tomorrow what could be done today, you'll clog your mind up with worrying thoughts about what you haven't done and render yourself ineffective, so tell yourself to 'do it now' and get started right away.

If procrastination is a problem for you, write the affirmation, **'DO IT NOW'** on small cards and sticky notes and paste them all over the house, your car, office, anywhere you'll see them. Repeat these words to yourself at every opportunity. You'll soon notice a difference as your subconscious brings your behaviour into line.

232

Five ways to overcome procrastination:

1   Ask yourself, 'When would *now* be the best time to start?'

2   The **salami technique** – break tasks down into thin slices and 'eat' one slice at a time.

3   The **worst first** approach – do the most unpleasant jobs first. Don't put them off: the chances are that what you put off now you will also put off later, and what you put off today you will also put off tomorrow.

4   Write a balance sheet – list all the reasons why you've been procrastinating on the left side of a piece of paper, and all the benefits of getting the job done on the right. Read it through several times and then get started. This helps you appreciate the advantages of doing it now.

5   The **leading task** – is there one thing which, if you did it, would break into the log jam? If so, do it now.

233

Face up to your fears. An ancient sage said, 'Try once to get over the fear of doing something; try twice to enable you to learn to do it well; try three times to see if you like doing it or not.'

Courageous people are not genetically resistant to fear. They feel it just like everyone else, but they don't let it hold them back. Fears are a part of being human – accept them. Our brains and bodies do not like risk; it makes them feel uncomfortable.

Confront your fears. Be realistic about what to expect. Think of the worst that could happen and put a coping strategy in place in case it comes about. And think of what could go right too – there are always two sides to every coin.

To help you overcome a fear, ask yourself: 'How would the rest of my life be better if I overcame this fear?' Imagine being free of the fear forever. Doesn't that feel good?

234

Three common fears:

1   Fear of failure is one of the most common fears, even among people who have a clear vision and appreciate the rewards that success would bring. Sufferers worry that all their hard work and commitment will come to nothing, or some disaster will befall them, such as being cheated or going bankrupt. Many have such a strong fear of failure that they're too scared to even try.

Consider failure as part of the learning process, a stepping stone to success. Sometimes the failure to achieve one goal leads to even better things in most surprising ways.

If you suffer from fear of failure, write this sentence at the top of a piece of paper:

'What I fear most about failure is ....'

Quickly write six to ten responses to this sentence. Don't think too hard, just jot down what comes into your head. Examine what you've written. How do you feel about 'failure' now?

2   Others have just as great a fear of success. They fear that it would bring more responsibilities, or they wouldn't be able to cope with the stress, or would lose touch with their family and friends, or have less time to spend on their hobbies and interests, etc.

Some people don't even want their problems solved, because they fear they'll end up with an even bigger problem. A promotion, for instance, can solve money problems, but bring increased stress and responsibility. Fear of success is sometimes the fear of failure masked – 'I can succeed so far, but then I'll fail.'

Fear of success is harder to identify because it is often subconscious. The best way to recognise whether it is a problem for you is to relax into alpha and ask yourself, 'How do I feel about success?' Then monitor your physiology carefully. A tight feeling in the stomach, chest or throat could reveal a hidden fear.

3   The third major fear is fear of ridicule, and it is one of the strongest fears. It can be very disheartening when friends and colleagues mock your efforts.

People who have new ideas are often derided or even persecuted, and many are put off. Successful people, however, are not. For instance, Brunel was widely thought to be an idiot for thinking that iron ships could actually float, Bob Dylan was mocked for his singing voice, and Sylvester Styllone for his wooden acting; Marconi was laughed at for trying to transmit sound without using wires.

Fear of ridicule can prevent people taking risks, branching out and ignoring the conventional wisdom of the time. This is what Albert Einstein meant when he wrote, 'Great spirits have always encountered violent opposition from mediocre minds.'

Most people dread losing face, but if you worry too much about what other people think, you'll take too much notice of ill informed individuals who are all too ready to dismiss new ideas.

Has fear of ridicule ever stopped you chasing a dream? In what way? How will you handle similar situations in the future?

235

Do something every day. Success consists of many small daily victories. Even if you only spend ten minutes a day on a project, you're making progress. Just half an hour a day, say, reading up on your chosen subject makes you an expert within a year compared with 98 per cent of the population! So don't be afraid to take the phone off the hook and put a 'do not disturb' sign on your door when you want to be left alone. The main thing is you will be living your dream, and the more you live it, the sooner it will become reality.

■ What can you do each morning to get your day off to a good start?

■ What can you do each day to keep the momentum going?

236

Here are two useful questions to ask yourself at regular intervals every day:

1 What is my intention in doing what I am doing right now?

2 Does it contribute to my success and happiness?

237

Small steps: you can't reach the top of a ladder in one huge leap – you must climb one rung at a time. Major goals must be broken down into bite-size chunks, then tackled one chunk at a time. Small steps make the task less intimidating.

When I wrote this book I started by making a mind map™, then a broad plan which I broke down into themes, then sections. I wrote one section at a time, keeping in mind the overall plan. This made it manageable. If I had allowed my mind to dwell on the enormity of the task – the more than 200 pages, 365 hints and 55,000 words of it, I could easily have been overwhelmed.

Take the right small steps and the big ones take care of themselves.

238

Big steps: however, sometimes it's necessary to take big steps. As David Lloyd George famously pointed out, 'Don't be afraid to take a big step if one is indicated. You can't cross a chasm in two small jumps.'

Do you know anyone who has taken a leap of faith? How did it work out?

Have you? Did it achieve what you wanted? Would you do it again?

239

Going the extra mile means giving that bit extra. For instance, if you run a sweet store, throw a few extra sweets into the bag. If a cafe owner, offer a free biscuit with each cup of coffee. If in a relationship, do more than your partner expects of you and he or she will respond in many wonderful ways.

If you're in business, when you give more than expected two things happen:

- Your customers come back for more, recognising the 'added value' you offer.

- They recommend you to others. Word of mouth advertising is the cheapest and also the most effective. A good reputation is the least tangible business asset, but easily the most valuable.

In business (as in other areas of life) if you look for shortcuts that do not give genuine value for money as a means of making a fast buck, you'll almost certainly fail. Similarly in your personal life a little extra thoughtfulness, generosity and support pay dividends for all concerned.

240

Teamwork: few prosper without working effectively with others. Few relationships succeed without a sense of partnership. In team sports it is often those who work best as a team who are victorious, rather than the most talented group of individuals.

The point is well made in a story told to me by an elderly uncle. As a young merchant seaman during the Second World War he witnessed a ship's painter taking exception to a bowler hatted clerk who was barking out his orders without so much as a 'please' or 'thank you'. 'Excuse me,' demanded the painter, pointing to a small table, 'which of the legs on that table is the most important?' The pompous man grunted and turned away.

Working with a team enables you to:

■ Complement your own abilities, knowledge and skills and plug the gaps in areas where you're relatively weak.

■ Generate more, and better, ideas.

■ Have access to contacts and resources you do not have.

■ Achieve more as a team than operating as separate individuals – this is the benefit of 'synergy' (or the '2 + 2 = 5' effect).

■ Strengthen your resolve through sharing values and purpose.

A team can be either formal or informal. It may meet together on a regular basis, or never meet at all. What matters is that you seek out people who can help and be prepared to ask for advice.

241

Reward your helpers: if you have the support of a team, make sure that everyone benefits. Let them share your success. Few people are willing to play in a band where the leader wants all the solos.

Many businesses are built on the idea that you can hire another person's labour and pay them as little as it takes to motivate them and retain their services. Employers frequently argue that they cannot afford to pay above the market rate, however meagre, because they would be driven out of business by spiralling costs. Although there is some truth in this, companies that pay above the odds tend to attract a better calibre of employee and retain their services longer. It is also, to some extent, a matter of conscience. Is it fair to claim all the credit for ourselves when we owe our success to the cooperation of others? People lose interest when they feel used.

The remuneration you offer may be financial and material, but praise, recognition, special treats and so on are just as important. Everyone appreciates a few kind words and recognition of a job well done.

242

Don't be a **DOPE**: 'driven by other people's expectations'.

Much of what happens to us in life is determined by the people we associate with on a daily basis. We begin to think, behave, move and talk like them. We are all influenced by people around us, which is why drug addicts and alcoholics tend to mix with other drug addicts and alcoholics, and muggers with other muggers.

Seek out people who have a sense of purpose and a vision of their own. Choose your friends carefully and mix, as far as possible, with kindred spirits. Go to workshops about health, happiness and success.

If you are ever tempted to give up because others pour scorn, remember Wim Ouboter, the man who invented the Micro skate scooter. When he made his first prototype friends and family thought he was crazy. 'I looked so funny that people laughed at me,' he said, 'even my closest friends.'

He tried to franchise it, but was greeted with scepticism and disbelief. 'Lots of people said it wouldn't sell. They thought it was a toy, and I was a bit of a joke.' He went ahead anyway, and now, so far, over five million have been sold around the world.

243

List the attributes of the people with whom you should associate in order to be happier and achieve your goals.

Examine your list. Do you know anyone like this? How could you spend more time in their company and let some of their magic rub off on you?

244

Avoid 'sabotage friends'. These are the ones who buy you chocolate when you're on a diet, try to tempt you out drinking when you want to get your work done, or offer you cigarettes when you're trying to give up.

Your efforts to improve your life can easily highlight problems in others' lives. They feel threatened, but their behaviour is more about how they feel about themselves than what they think of you. Don't get sucked in. Hold fast to your principles and they can only make you stronger.

Keep your plans confidential, apart from sharing them with go-ahead individuals who can support you, and don't listen to those who say it can't be done. How can anyone else know what's right for you?

■ Are there people in your life from whom you need to distance yourself?

■ If you prefer to follow the crowd, remember the word 'fashion' often goes with 'victim'.

245

Be willing to learn from others. There isn't a soul on this planet from whom you cannot learn something of value. The hard part is recognising who, and in what form the message is delivered, but when you keep your wits about you they're not too hard to spot.

Author John McCormack tells how, as a young man, he was idling away his time on the beach, unsure what to do with his life, when he came across an elderly man. At first he thought he was a tramp, but they struck up a conversation and John discovered that he was a former Eastern European refugee who had arrived in the USA as a young man, penniless and unable to speak a word of English. He had established a business in an unglamorous trade and become a multimillionaire. The two became friends, and over time the old man passed on a wealth of wisdom and experience which set McCormack on the road to financial success of his own.

Everyone you meet has something to teach you, but you won't find out what it is unless you're prepared to suspend judgement and listen!

246

A balanced life: 'all work and no joy makes Jack a dull boy,' says the old proverb, but what place should work occupy in our lives compared with, say, family and leisure time? How can busy people manage their careers so they have the time and energy they need for other things?

Keep things in perspective. Pleasure comes not from doing huge amounts of work, but from doing it with joy and creativity. Don't be so preoccupied with achievement that you miss out on the pleasures of living in the moment. The wonder of a beautiful sunset, the miracle of bird song, the joy of laughter, playing with a small child, watching the tides roll in and so on can never be truly experienced when your mind is constantly engrossed in some hypothetical future.

Time management

Time is your most important resource and the most valuable. It is also the most democratic – you have exactly the same amount of time each day as everybody else – the only difference is in how you use it.

Unlike money, you can't save time to spend another day; once it's gone, it's gone and you can never get it back. And no matter how much time you've wasted in the past, you've still got now, today, tomorrow and the day after that…

247

How much time do you have? Take your present age and subtract it from 80. (If you're already older than 80 or think you're likely to live longer than this, choose a greater number.) Multiply by 12. For example, if you're 45, 80 – 45 = 35 x 12 = 420.

This is the number of months you're likely to have left in this life. How quickly the months go by! A sobering thought, isn't it?

248

Do you use your time wisely? Every moment of each day is either used well or wasted. How much of your time do you use productively?

■ All of it?

■ Most of it?

■ Very little?

NB: relaxation and time for pleasure are definitely *not* a waste, but watching mindless TV is!

249

Time management is defined as doing the right thing in the right way at the right time.

All high achievers use their time well. They work when they work, relax when they relax and know how to pace themselves. Take a leaf out of their book and make full use of this priceless resource. Make the best use of every moment and never 'kill' time – it's much too precious!

250

The golden rule in time management is to put first things first. Do things in order of importance and avoid wasting time on the non-essential. Devote as much time as you can to activities that contribute the most to your happiness and success.

Ask yourself, 'What one thing could I do, that I'm not currently doing, and which, if I did it regularly would make the biggest difference to my life?' This is your number one priority.

251

In his book *The Seven Habits of Highly Effective People* Dr Stephen Covey suggests that you classify things to do under four headings:

	Important	Not important
Urgent	Urgent and important	Urgent but not important
Not urgent	Important but not urgent	Not urgent and not important

Dr Covey points out that many of us get so bogged down with the unimportant and non-urgent that we lose sight of what really matters – the important and urgent items in the top left-hand cell.

He also points out that the important but non-urgent items in the bottom left hand cell are usually those that build your future. Allocate some time to these every day. They may do little to ease your workload today but map the course of your life in the longer term.

The 'to do' list

Keeping an ongoing 'to do' list is essential for making the best use of your time. Correct use of the 'to do' list can immediately increase your productivity by up to a third.

252

Use a small notebook or loose leaf pad for your 'to do' list. Carry it around with you and update it continually. When you have a new task to complete, add it to your list. When you have completed a task, cross it off.

253

Each evening make a list of what you intend to do the following day. Mark each item either urgent or non-urgent, and either important or unimportant and plot on Dr Covey's matrix. Make sure you include everything – working activities, recreation, personal development, household duties, etc.

Now rank all items, the most important first. Focus on the important and the urgent. Also, pay attention to the important but non-urgent. Put off everything else. You'll be amazed how many minor problems resolve themselves if you ignore them for a while.

Either write the rankings on your list in your notebook, or transfer them, in rank order, to a sheet such as the one opposite (if you wish, photocopy it for your use).

Urgent? (tick)	Things to do today Date	Done? (tick)
	1	
	2	
	3	
	4	
	5	
	6	
	7	
	8	
	9	
	10	

254 Each day, work down your list tackling one task at a time. Complete each item before moving on to the next.

Develop a sense of urgency. When something must be done, don't put it off. Do it now. As you finish a task, cross it off. If you don't get everything done today, add it to tomorrow's list (if it's still important enough).

At the end of each day, carry out an evening review. Cross off anything you haven't done which no longer needs doing (i.e. because events have overtaken you). Add in anything that needs to be added. Then start the cycle again.

255

Remember – and this is vital – to focus on the most important, not the most pleasant. Postponing important tasks simply because they are unpleasant clogs the brain, reduces your creativity and gets you bogged down in trivialities. Moreover, tasks rarely get more pleasant by being postponed.

256

Do things well enough. Avoid exaggerated perfectionism. Know when 'good enough' is 'good enough'. (This is one of the best time-saving hints of all.)

If this is hard for you, it may be something to do with your upbringing. Were your parents or other adult caretakers perfectionists?

257

Tackle the most demanding jobs, those that require maximum energy, attention and brain capacity, when you're at your best. When we work with our body's natural rhythms, we are more productive and less likely to suffer the adverse effects of stress. Use those times when your brain can only cope with small things to get those boring, routine tasks done.

258

Making the best use of your time does not mean losing your spontaneity. If an opportunity comes up to do something you wouldn't normally do or hadn't planned for, go for it; you may not get another chance. If the weather's good and you have a chance to take a walk by the sea, do it. If a friend calls round and invites you out for a drink, go for it. These moments are precious and add enormously to your quality of life – and you can always catch up on your work later.

Taking good care of yourself

You'll never reach your potential nor enjoy life to the full if you're not up to it physically. Looking after your body is very important. How healthy are you? What kind of fuel do you put into your body? Do you pickle your brain and liver with alcohol? Clog your arteries with fat and greasy fried junk food? Do you exercise regularly? Are you slim and full of energy, or overweight and sluggish? Do you puff going up a flight of stairs?

The World Health Organisation defines 'health' as:

> 'A positive state of equilibrium on a physical, mental and social level,
> not merely the absence of disease or disability.'

It is obvious from this definition that good health demands a holistic approach incorporating physical factors (i.e. nutrition, exercise, breathing, sleep, etc) and the psychological. You need plenty of energy. You also need to be able to handle the stresses of life with calmness and composure.

Everyone knows what is required to be healthy – good food, clean air, exercise, plenty of the right fluids, sleep and relaxation – but, as we've said before, knowing what is to be done but not actually doing it is like hoping to get better merely by reading the label on the medicine bottle!

259 Sit quietly for a few minutes and experience the flow of energy through your body. Just stay calm and still, and observe.

Now contemplate the benefits of optimum health, and promise yourself that you will do whatever you can to achieve the best possible level of health and vitality that is available to you.

260 Breath – the life force. It's impossible to underestimate the importance of the breath. A plentiful supply of fresh air is essential for health, energy, vitality and emotional wellbeing. You can go a month without food, a week without water, but less than five minutes without oxygen.

Slow, deep breathing has a calming and energising effect on mind and body. Deep breathing also activates the lymphatic system, which removes waste products and dead cells from the body. Your lungs eliminate 60–70 per cent of the toxins from the body. If you want to maximise your energy, learn to breathe correctly. Until you try it, you won't believe the difference it makes.

Practise the **complete breath**. Stand or sit erect. Inhale through your nose right into the pit of your stomach. Fill your lungs entirely, expanding your ribs and stomach outward. Hold for four seconds. Breathe out through your mouth by contracting your stomach muscles (if it helps, press on the abdomen) and expelling the air as though you were squeezing it out of a balloon. Repeat several times with a continuous flowing action.

If you feel dizzy, don't worry, sit down until the feeling has gone: it's merely that your brain probably isn't use to receiving this amount of oxygen.

261

Nutrition: one of the keys to good health and vitality is to eat healthily. Cultivate a taste for fresh vegetables, fruit and whole grains. If you eat meat, choose white meats (such as chicken) and fish. Avoid as much as possible sugary foods, excessive dairy products, white flour, and chemically preserved and processed foods.

A natural diet of whole grains, fruit and vegetables is cheaper and healthier than the conventional diet and can provide more than enough protein for the average person's needs.

Write down everything that has passed your lips in the last 24 hours. Then tick anything that falls into the following categories:

Fresh fruit and vegetables
Salads
Whole grains
White meat or fish
High protein foods such as nuts or pulses
Fruit juices, mineral water, herbal teas

What proportion of your total intake have you circled?

More than 80 per cent	Excellent!
50 to 80 per cent	Good
20 to 49 per cent	Room for improvement
Less than 20 per cent	Suicide!

262

Fluids: the best fluids are fruit and vegetable juices, natural mineral water and herbal teas. These all thin the blood, flush out the toxins and help prevent the body being poisoned by its own waste matter. Animal milks and beers should be regarded as foods rather than liquids.

Drink lots of water. Water makes up three quarters of the human body, and brain tissue consists of over 80 per cent water. Drink three to four pints of good quality water every day and keep sipping throughout the day.

263

Regular exercise:

- Increases energy and stamina.

- Increases resistance to disease.

- Lowers cholesterol levels.

- Promotes deeper, more satisfying sleep.

- Promotes a more youthful appearance.

- Makes you sweat, which cleanses and revitalises.

- Helps you lose weight and keep it off.

- Makes the heart more efficient.

- Brings a multitude of psychological benefits, including increased self-confidence, better concentration, improved memory and greater resilience to depression and stress.

The kinds and amounts of exercise needed to reap such rewards are well within the reach of most people, even if they haven't exercised regularly for years. As little as 30 minutes rapid walking four times a week can provide up to ten years of rejuvenation.

Do what you enjoy. Also, make discreet adjustments to your lifestyle. Walk or cycle instead of using motorised transport. Use the stairs instead of the lift – stair climbing is excellent aerobic exercise.

Important: if you haven't exercised regularly for several years, have a check up with your doctor before taking up strenuous activity.

264

Regular sleep is vital. Sleep deprivation wrecks body and mind. Warning signs include:

- Poor concentration.

- Irritability.

- Tiredness (in the morning – it's OK to be tired at the end of the day).

Most of us need six to eight hours per night, preferably at regular times. Also, respect your biorhythms. Each of us has a personal rhythm that is tied to our bodily needs. Some of us are at our best in the morning, some in the evening, some at night. Which of these describe you?

- I love getting up early.

- I feel sluggish in the mornings.

- I function best in the afternoon.

- I'm at my best in the evening.

- I'm a night owl.

You'll function best when you don't try to fight your personal rhythm.

265

Relaxation is also essential. It's extremely beneficial for your physical and mental health, and the leading safeguard against stress.

Intermittent tension does no harm at all, but sustained muscle tension can have harmful effects. Even clenching your fist can significantly raise your blood pressure. We need to learn about the state of the muscles and recognise the difference between a tense muscle and one that is soft and relaxed.

Practise deep relaxation techniques. Treat yourself to an occasional massage, aromatherapy, sauna, reflexology, hydrotherapy, manicure – whatever you fancy. Above all, don't feel guilty; you deserve it!

266

Poor posture restricts breathing, induces muscle tension and sometimes causes undesirable changes in bone and muscle structure. For example, if you persistently carry two heavy shopping bags in one hand, you will put your spine out of balance; far better to carry one in each hand to even the load.

Many activities can cause neck and back strain: washing up, crouching over a desk, using a vacuum cleaner, lifting heavy objects, etc. Any position held long enough will cause tension and discomfort. None of this need be a problem for you if you learn to carry and use your body correctly.

Stand in a relaxed way with your shoulders, hips and ankles in line. Keep your spine straight, shoulders dropped and relaxed, your head slightly forward and up (so you could balance a book on it). Think of the neck as being free, and allow the back to lengthen and widen.

Sit with your back straight, with your feet on the floor, uncrossed. If you are engaged in repetitive work, take mini-breaks to help prevent repetitive strain injury.

267

Ageing: age isn't just a matter of how many years you've lived. This is merely your *chronological* age. But what about your *biological* age, as measured in terms of cellular processes and critical life signs, or your *psychological* age – the age you feel you are? Only one of these is fixed; the other two can be influenced by a healthy attitude and healthy lifestyle.

The most significant is your psychological age, which has been proven to have a profound influence on your biological age. Adopting a more positive attitude and a healthier lifestyle can reduce your biological age considerably.

What age were you when you were at your most energetic? Aim to 'live' this age. Talk, dress, think and *be* that age. If you do it really well, people will begin to think you are, and so will you!

Step six: summing up

Thinking and dreaming won't take you closer to achieving your goals. Only action will.

Effective action demands accepting personal responsibility, staying focused, knowing what's important and what is not, being willing to listen and learn, overcoming procrastination and, in some cases, facing up to your fears. It also means making the best use of your time and, if your goal is a particularly challenging one, hard work and discipline.

Happiness and success require you to find what you love doing and put your heart and soul into it. They require you to make a valuable contribution to the lives of others. Then hard work doesn't seem so bad; on the contrary – it's enjoyable and fulfilling.

8   Step seven: monitoring your progress

> *What does not destroy me makes me stronger.*
>
> **Friedrich Nietzsche**

In self-coaching there is no such thing as failure – only actions and their consequences. Successful people make mistakes of course, but they also have an unwavering determination to keep trying until they've achieved their objectives. They continually assess whether they're still on the right track. If they are, they keep going. If not, they make adjustments to avoid making the same mistakes again.

268   Include frequent progress reviews. Advancement towards your goals should be monitored continually: short-term goals on a daily basis, medium-term weekly and long-term monthly or quarterly. Plot your review dates in your diary, on your wall chart or in your Self-Coaching Journal.

Continually ask yourself:

- What's going really well for me right now?

- What could I build on?

- What could I usefully do more of?

- What could I make even better?

269

Although it's important to think positively, you mustn't kid yourself that you're making progress when you're not. If you're making headway – fine. Keep going. Carry out some fine-tuning if necessary.

But if you're not, find out where you're going wrong and make adjustments. And remember, it's OK to make mistakes: hardly anyone gets it right first time. Make *new* mistakes, *better* mistakes – just don't keep making the *same* mistakes. That's how you grow.

If it's not working at all, try something different. The more things you try, the more likely you are to hit upon the right thing at the right time. Sooner or later you *will* find the right way.

270

Expect problems, setbacks and difficulties. There has never been, nor will there ever be, a life free from problems. Problems are an unavoidable part of human experience.

It is not your problems but how you deal with them that determines the direction of your life. You won't feel good about yourself unless you have a healthy attitude towards problems. Usually it's your response to a problem as much as the problem itself that determines the outcome. Accepting this puts you in the right frame of mind to find solutions.

Reflect on this: have you ever faced a major problem that seemed terrible at the time, that you now look back on and think, 'I learned a lot from that'? You handled it. Perhaps you surprised yourself, and now thanks to this, you feel more confident. Make a note in your Self-Coaching Journal of how you would react if that kind of situation happened again.

271

It is not our problems which distress us, but our lack of faith in our ability to solve them. Problems may initially appear as insurmountable obstacles, but in the long term they are stepping stones, lessons waiting to be learned. Often what appears to be a dead end turns out to be merely a bend in the road. You *can* solve problems. You've already solved thousands.

Frequently, opportunities come our way disguised as problems. All it takes is a subtle change in thinking to make the most of them.

Do you see problems as potential opportunities? If not, what can you do to take a more constructive view?

272

Eight ways to approach a problem:

1   Write it down. Look at it as if it were a puzzle in a magazine. Problems often appear less threatening once put down on paper.

2   Focus your mind on finding a solution. Spend no more than 20 per cent of your time defining the problem, and 80 per cent on thinking about the solution.

3   Let go of self-pitying self-talk and negative questions. Ask: 'What can I do to solve this problem?' 'How can I turn it to my advantage?' 'What more do I need to know?' and so on. These great questions get your subconscious working for rather than against you.

4   Don't exaggerate the problem. Problems are blown up by anxious thoughts, anger, guilt and looking for someone or something to blame.

5   Don't underestimate the problem either, nor your capacity to deal with it. Many problems are handled badly because they aren't taken seriously enough. Don't delude yourself. See reality as it is.

6   Take action now. You solve problems by doing something about them now, not in the future.

7   Don't be too proud to ask for help. You'll find people love to lend a hand. It makes them feel useful and boosts their self-esteem.

8   If all else fails, ask your intuitive mind for guidance (see pages 94–95).

273

Stay flexible – flexibility does not mean feebleness. The tree that is strong and pliant enough to sway with the wind best weathers the storm. So hang in there and be prepared to change your approach if necessary.

Sometimes things happen you just can't help. A new boss arrives, reorganises the department and you're made redundant. The company is taken over by a competitor, slims down and closes your premises. You're given the choice of relocating to a part of the country where you don't want to go, or lose your job. Your wife has a nervous breakdown, gives up her job and announces she has been having an affair. Your daughter announces that she is hooked on heroin. What can you do?

First, don't blame yourself if this happens. Second, reaffirm that you always have choices, even if some are not always immediately apparent.

274

Learn from your failures. Composer Igor Stravinsky echoed millions of wise individuals when he said, 'I have learned throughout my life chiefly through my mistakes and pursuits of false assumptions, not by my exposure to founts of wisdom and knowledge.'

Learn from all your so-called failures. From the moment we're born life presents us with a series of learning curves, each building on the other. A baby has to fall many times before walking, and, as adults, sometimes we feel as if we're about to topple over before recovering our balance and getting back on our feet again. Failing at something doesn't make us a failure as a person. The only real failure is giving up or not trying at all.

Successful people see setbacks as valuable lessons, teaching them about what they need to alter within themselves so they can achieve what they want. This explains why so many of them ultimately bounce back completely transformed.

Every setback contains within it the seeds of success, providing you can spot them. Deal with problems as they arise and turn difficulties to your advantage. Hardly anyone gets everything right first time.

275 If you're sure you've found the right goals, have applied all four parts of the ITIA formula, tried your hardest and your efforts are still not bearing fruit, ask yourself candidly:

■ What am I unwilling to do?

■ What is it that I am not facing up to? Not changing? Not giving up?

■ What am I unwilling to do to achieve my goal?

Lack of success is often the result of being unwilling to do *everything* that is required. One final step has yet to be taken. For example, many complementary therapists struggle to establish their practices despite being well qualified and competent at their chosen therapy. In nearly every case, their failure is due to their unwillingness to get involved in the business side of things, especially marketing and promoting themselves.

If you're aware of something you're unwilling to do that is holding you back, there's only one sensible solution. Make a plan, apply the ITIA formula and Eight Steps and start right now.

Step seven: summing up

The most successful individuals in whatever field understand that there is no such thing as failure – only actions and their consequences. They see setbacks as learning opportunities, stepping stones to success.

Welcome problems, setbacks and difficulties. Embrace the learning opportunities they offer. But keep your feet on the ground; don't deceive yourself into thinking you're making progress when you're not. (Equally, don't talk yourself into thinking you're not making progress when you are.)

If what you do works, do more of it, do it more often, do it for longer, do it on a bigger scale. If it doesn't, think again. Stay flexible, be willing to adjust your strategy, or, if necessary, go back to square one and start again.

9 Step eight: plugging into the power of persistence

> *Thousands of people have talent. I might as well congratulate you for having eyes in your head. The one and only thing that counts is, do you have staying power?*
>
> **Noel Coward**

Whatever your aptitudes and ambitions, there is no substitute for the twin attributes of patience and persistence. Few of us get far without them in any area of life.

History is littered with examples of people who've given up when with just a little more effort they could have succeeded. There are also countless examples of courageous and far-sighted individuals who persisted against the odds.

One was Charles Darrow. When he sent his idea for a new game to Parker Brother, they turned it down. They cited 52 reasons why the game would never sell, including the 'fact' that nobody would be interested in a game about property trading. But Darrow was persistent and eventually won them over. His game, Monopoly, became the best selling game of the twentieth century.

The Japanese have a saying, 'Fall down seven times, stand up eight.' Have you the strength and determination to get up each time you fall? Don't be discouraged; look upon every problem as a challenge to be faced and overcome. And whatever happens, stay on purpose. If it's right for you, and you apply the right principles, everything *will* work out.

276

Patience: lasting results take time, especially if the goal is a challenging one. The creative process is a little like gardening: take care of the sowing and you will get results. Be patient, have faith and let nature do its work.

Often you don't know how well it's going until months or years later, and you can't keep pulling a young plant up by the roots to check whether it's still growing.

Once you've planted the seeds there will be times when you'll have to work hard, and times when it is better to sit back, observe and be patient. Simply do the best you can each day.

If you apply the right principles, you can rest assured that you will get results. You may even far exceed your expectations. So what if you don't succeed first time? The obstacles don't grow any bigger – but you do!

> *On the whole, it is patience which makes the final difference between those who succeed or fail; in all things. All the greatest people have it in infinite degree, and among the less, the patient weak ones always conquer the impatient strong.*
>
> **John Ruskin**

277

An essential affirmation:

So long as there is breath in my body, I will persevere.
I know the great secret of success – if I persist, I will succeed.

Step eight: summing up

All the preceding seven steps will come to nothing if you give up at the first sign of difficulty or disappointment. Naturally some of your smaller, short-term goals may be achieved quickly and fairly easily, but the bigger goals, the long-term ones that make the biggest difference, will inevitably take time and require more effort.

This applies especially to the mental conditioning and character forming techniques in Steps two and three. Remember, these are the main 'causes' that shape your life. Deep-seated patterns are unlikely to change overnight, but they do change (and sometimes quicker than you imagine) if you persist.

Lasting change takes time, and when the going gets tough remember how much better you feel when you achieve something worthwhile by sticking at it. So press on. Nothing can take the place of patience and persistence.

10 The art of relating

> *It is the individual who is not interested in his fellow men who has the greatest difficulties in life and provides the greatest injury to others. It is from among such individuals that all human failures spring.*
>
> **Alfred Adler**

People skills are a prerequisite of happiness and success. They are indispensable in every area of life.

Human beings are social animals. We feel empty and hollow without fulfilling relationships. We need friends to care and be cared for and in our working lives the ability to get on with a wide variety of people is an important factor in career success. Would you like to be great with people, to make friends easily, to be the sort of person others love to be around?

To some, it comes naturally. They had the advantage of good role models when they were young. Others had a poor start but learned through experience. If you consider yourself to be shy and awkward with people, you too can learn. The skills are easily acquired; an attractive personality is easily within the reach of everyone who is willing to practise a few attitudes and skills.

Of course, your prime relationship is with yourself, and this is the springboard for all your other relationships. Your attitude to yourself is like a pair of coloured spectacles through which you view everyone (and everything) else. That's why some people constantly attract inconsiderate, indifferent, even abusive partners who are genuinely incapable of loving them – but they don't believe deep down that they are worthy of anyone better. Psychotherapists' appointment diaries are full of such people.

There are eight basic laws governing your relationships. They apply to your relationship with your partner or spouse, your children, friends, neighbours, work colleagues… even complete strangers. Understanding and mastering these principles will help you to get on with everyone.

278

Think of someone with whom you like spending time. What is it about them you like? How do they treat you? How do they talk? Behave? How could you 'model' this person to improve your own interpersonal skills (see 209)?

People principle no 1: at its most basic level, a relationship is about a mutual fulfilling of needs.

279

If you fulfil another's needs, they want to maintain and deepen their relationship with you. Think about it – would you want to spend time with someone who always takes without giving anything in return?

These needs can be physical, practical or (more usually) emotional. Attention, loyalty, fun, affection, companionship, moral support, appreciation and so on are basic to human survival.

280

Consider your own relationship needs. Take a pen and paper and write down at least ten things you look for in your (a) intimate relationships, (b) social relationships, (c) business and work-related relationships in the grid opposite.

Ten things I look for in my **intimate** relationships	Ten things I look for in my **social** relationships	Ten things I look for in my **business/work** relationships
1		
2		
3		
4		
5		
6		
7		
8		
9		
10		

281 What people want from relationships. People enter into relationships primarily because they want to feel good. They want to feel noticed, valued and safe. In addition, most of us want:

■ To be heard.

■ Recognition.

■ Approval and appreciation.

■ Common purpose and values.

■ Loyalty.

■ Integrity and trust.

- Practical support.

- Respect for their individuality.

- Fun, humour and play.

Do you agree with this list? Can you add more 'wants' of your own?

282

What people don't want from relationships. Among the most common dislikes are:

- Criticism.

- Dishonesty/deceit.

- Secrecy/aloofness.

- Untrustworthiness.

- Antagonistic/confrontational behaviour.

- Being gossiped about.

- Bullying.

- Scheming and manipulation.

- Complaining.

Do you agree with this list? Can you add a few more 'don't wants' of your own?

283

Choose someone with whom you either have a relationship (business, social or personal), or would like one.

- What do you think they want from their relationship with you?

- How far are you meeting these needs at present?

- What could you do to meet them more effectively?

People principle no 2: if you want a relationship to succeed, take responsibility.

284

Take responsibility. If you want a relationship – any relationship – to succeed, approach it with the attitude of putting something in rather than getting something out. Make them feel appreciated and important. Then maybe they'll want to do the same for you.

Don't blame others if a relationship is not going well; take responsibility for putting it right. Naturally there are times when others are unreasonable and just too demanding, in which case you must decide how far you're willing to go. But remember, there are two sides to every coin.

285

Relationships as a mirror. Once you accept that your relationship with yourself is the basis of your relationships, then you realise that others are like a mirror, reflecting back to you the way you are. Your thoughts and feelings about other human beings say a lot more about what is inside you than what is inside them.

For instance, if you're the kind of person who thinks people are out to get you, it's probably because you think that way yourself; if you're the jealous sort, it says a lot more about your insecurities than the person you're jealous of. We all tend to project our internal conflicts onto others.

When you become aware of this, you're on the way to genuine change. No more snapping at the children because you've had a hard day at work; no more blaming your partner for your own deficiencies. No more complaining about the boss or accusing him or her of being unfair for not promoting you. You place the responsibility exactly where it lies – with yourself.

People principle no 3: unless you have a genuine interest in others, your relationships will never be wholly satisfactory.

286

A negative attitude inevitably manifests in the way you conduct yourself, especially a negative attitude to the people around you. You soon alienate most of them; they start to mistrust and avoid you. If your work involves serving the public, you lose business – who'd want to buy from someone who seems devious, sour or surly?

You'll only get people's backs up if you constantly judge and criticise, gloat, blame others when the problem lies with you, or fall into self-pity when things go wrong. No one wants to be around a person like that.

Are you genuinely interested in other people? With a genuine interest in other people all your relationships can become enormously gratifying.

287

Reflect on your attitude to people.

■ Do you like people?

■ Do they like you?

■ Do you believe people are unfair to you?

■ Do you readily blame others when things go wrong?

■ Do you have dozens of rewarding friendships? Or very few?

List any improvements to your attitude that you would like to make. Adopt the attitude 'I'll make everyone glad they talked to me!'

 *You can make more friends in two months by becoming interested in other people than you can in two years by trying to get other people interested in you.*

Dale Carnegie

People principle no 4: know that it is impossible to fake an interest in others.

288

In relationships you get back what you give out. You telegraph your
inner feelings in many subtle ways – posture, facial expression, tone of
voice, gesture, etc – so if you're only pretending to be interested in
others, they know. (If not consciously, your indifference registers
*sub*consciously.)

The most popular people genuinely like and care for others. They
give off positive 'vibes'.

Develop a *bona fide*, open, caring and friendly attitude. Let it
emanate from the inside-out to everyone you meet.

289

Every time you meet someone – whether you know them or not –
silently wish them love, health, happiness and success.

After a month, take stock of the ways in which your relationships
have improved.

People principle no 5: listening and communication skills are the basis of
relationships. They are the basis of all relationships, the secret of popularity and, unless
your goal is to become a hermit, indispensable for a happy and successful life. That's
why most of the remainder of this book is devoted to them. They are crucial assets in
your pursuit of your goals.

People principle no 6: relate to others on an emotional level.

290

A major step in getting on well with people is to understand and respect
others' feelings no matter how unreasonable and groundless they seem.
This is not so difficult for some, but more problematic for individuals
who are guided mainly by the left brain.

Human beings are emotional creatures. We are more inclined to
respond emotionally than logically. Sometimes our emotional impulses
work to our advantage, but they can also spell disaster if, for example,
we dismiss another person's point of view because we don't like the
look of them, or we've heard something about them that we don't like.

People want to feel good. Knowing how to make others feel good about themselves emotionally is the key to good relationships.

Do you know how to make others feel good about themselves? If not, are you willing to find out and put what you discover into practice?

291

Here's the secret: whenever you have a choice to be *right* or be caring, choose *caring*. This means letting the occasional factual inaccuracy go. You don't have to compromise your integrity, just know when it is and is not important to take a stand.

292

Emotional intelligence: empathy, genuineness and positive regard. Dr Carl R. Rogers, the founder of 'person centred' counselling, believed that only three conditions have to be met for one person to support another emotionally. The only proviso is that they must be demonstrated in terms the other person can understand and relate to:

1   Acceptance.

2   Empathy.

3   Respect (positive regard).

These three are not difficult to learn, but must be practised.

293

Acceptance: everyone craves being acknowledged, appreciated and respected. Accepting another person unconditionally means acknowledging their opinions and feelings and their right to hold them – regardless of whether you agree. To *accept* another doesn't necessarily mean *liking* what the other person stands for.

Acceptance is the opposite of rejection, and also of:

■ Judging.

■ Criticising.

■ Accusing.

■ Mocking.

■ Moralising.

■ Disapproving.

From now on, work towards dropping these behaviours from your repertoire.

Empathy: empathy is the willingness and ability to see the world as if through another person's eyes rather than your own; to walk a mile in their moccasins, as the Native American proverb says.

Empathy involves:

■ Focused listening.

■ Being sensitive to another's feelings.

■ Understanding where they're coming from and why.

■ Responding to their needs and desires.

■ Communicating this in your words and actions.

Empathy requires patience, sensitivity, openness and trust. It cannot exist if either party feels threatened or wary.

The best way to demonstrate empathy is to listen with full attention.

Genuineness: good relationships can only be formed if both parties are genuine. This means being yourself, willing to open up and share your true feelings. People always know if you're being dishonest or deceitful.

You are still free to offer a different opinion to theirs if you wish, providing you express yourself constructively and with respect. You can always say 'I understand that's the way you feel, but I feel differently because...' without necessarily causing offence.

If you are genuinely interested in people, you will always be able to find something to talk about and leave them feeling better about themselves.

296

Finally, remember the 'as if' principle. We all know that emotions affect our actions – but it also works in reverse, your actions influence your emotions and those of others.

Be the kind of person others like having around. If you relax and smile, express yourself confidently, and are cheerful and pleasant no matter how you're feeling inside, you'll be making a valuable contribution to others' happiness and wellbeing.

People principle no 7: accept others as they are, not as you want them to be.

> " *The biggest thing that keeps people from having the relationships they want is that they're looking for a relationship to be the solution to their problems.*
>
> **Anthony Robbins**

297

Accepting others *as they are* is a vital key to harmonious relationships. Many people make the futile and frustrating effort to change others, especially those closest to them. What a waste of energy! You can't make another person something they're not, but you can try to relate to them better by changing your own mind-set.

This is a lesson some people take a long time to learn. When Jeannie's mean, neglectful and abusive husband stormed out, part of her was relieved. The other part was frightened she wouldn't be able to cope on her own.

'I want him back,' she said, 'but not as he used to be. I want him to be generous and considerate, and spend time with the children. And to listen to me.'

'What makes you think he'll change?' asked a friend.

'When he realises what he's done, he'll see the light. Otherwise, how can he ever be truly happy?'

Jeannie clung to her dream for nearly two years until she finally let go. Now she understands the 'if only Peter were more like Paul' pattern is common but pointless. If a person sees no need to change or doesn't want to, there's nothing you can do. Give others 'permission' to experience life the way they choose, otherwise you're condemning yourself to perhaps years of frustration. They're not going to change for you, any more than you'd change for them against your will.

298

For seven days, avoid judging other people. If another's values, beliefs, feelings, words or actions are different to your own, say to yourself 'I give you the space to experience life as you choose. It is not for me to judge you.'

After seven days, reflect. How do you feel? (Less irritable, perhaps?)

People principle no 8: work on yourself; become a better person and watch your relationships improve.

299

Your relationship with yourself is the basis of all your relationships. When your confidence and self-esteem are high you feel good about yourself and you also feel better about others. Then your relationships improve.

Work on your listening and communication skills. Expand your emotional intelligence. Cultivate an accepting, positive attitude to others. Be willing to change and to grow, to work on yourself, and become more tolerant and compassionate towards others.

Remember, what you give out you get back. Your relationships are the mirror which reflects back the way *you* are.

11 Communication skills

> *The most important single ingredient in the formula of success is knowing how to get along with people.*
>
> **Theodore Roosevelt**

It's almost impossible to understate the importance of good communication skills. They open doors, bring confidence, build relationships and smooth your progress towards your goals.

However, as we all know, communication can be fraught with difficulty. Say you want to put an idea across to another person:

1   First you must put your idea into words, limited tools which may not be adequate to express your true meaning, or draw a picture or diagram.

2   Let's suppose it's a verbal message. Once you've put it into words you must transmit them through some sort of channel – through the atmosphere, by telephone, letter, fax, e-mail and so on.

3   The other person must then hear or read the words accurately. Often there are barriers in place which interfere with reception, so he or she may only pick up a fraction of your intended meaning.

4   They must then interpret them. They may be confused by your words, or even consciously or unconsciously ignore part of the message.

It's no wonder that the message received can be very different from the original idea. Misunderstandings can be cleared up by asking for or providing feedback, but more often than not this doesn't happen.

Communication takes place in a variety of ways – face to face, in writing, electronically (telephone, radio, etc) and via e-mail and internet, etc. But we're going to concentrate on face to face interactions, because it is often these which are the most difficult.

300

The basics of good communication. In essence, becoming a good communicator is simple:

- First, be a good listener. Attentive listening is the basis of good communication skills. *Interested* people make *interesting* conversation.

- Next, have something good to say. You won't interest others unless you have something appealing to say. That's why the best conversationalists are those who lead a rich and varied life, keep themselves well informed and take an active interest in what's going on around them.

- Third, express yourself well. It's not just *what* you say, but *how* you say it; the language you use, anecdotes, your voice, your facial expressions, gestures, humour, etc.

- Finally, appeal to your listeners' emotions. Reason alone rarely makes friends or wins people over, or to put it another way, the 'head' never hears until the 'heart' has listened. Speak with passion. Let your eyes sparkle. Project warmth, empathy and caring. And remember: people are more likely to be won over by what you do than what you say (if the two are different you're branded a hypocrite) so make sure you 'walk your talk'.

301

The basic rule in all communication, whether you are transmitting or receiving, is to take responsibility. When you speak, make sure the other person has grasped your exact meaning; when listening, make sure that you fully understand what is said, no matter how clumsily expressed.

Before you can do this successfully you must be aware of the barriers that exist – and there may be many – and overcome them. There are both physical and psychological barriers:

■ Physical barriers include distance, noise interference, crackles on the telephone line, or any other external distraction. The listener may have poor hearing, or be deterred by the speaker's appearance or mannerisms.

■ Psychological barriers are more complicated and usually more subtle. True understanding is coloured by our attitudes and beliefs. We have a tendency to hear only what we want (or expect) to hear, and to screen out anything which we find unacceptable.

■ Another problem revolves around the meaning of words. The same word can mean very different things to different people. Words are merely symbols of ideas, which may conjure up a totally different mental image in the listener than that intended.

■ Emotional barriers are many and varied. People who feel insecure, anxious, suspicious, resentful, etc are prone to distorting what they say and hear. Also, if one of you feels tired, depressed, stressed or ill, they're less likely to pay attention.

■ Feelings about the situation or environment in which the communication takes place can also be important. For example, if you hate your job this could colour all your communications at work.

302

If your meaning is to be accurately understood it must be expressed in plain, clear, straightforward language. Memorise the mnemonic KISS:

Keep
It
Simple and
Straightforward.

There are no prizes for trying to impress with complicated language or jargon. On the contrary – you'll alienate a lot of people.

---

303 List your strengths and weaknesses as a communicator on the grid below.

My strengths as a communicator	My weaknesses as a communicator
....	....
....	....
....	....
....	....
....	....

Now reflect:

■ How can you make more of your strengths?

■ What do you need to do to overcome or eradicate your weaknesses?

■ What is likely to happen if you don't?

Active listening

Listening is a vital and often undervalued communication skill.

Listening is an active and conscious use of your hearing. Hearing is simply what happens when your ears pick up noise. It is a passive and unconscious use of your senses. But listening is intentional and deliberate.

Listening is the way you learn from others. It is also the way you show that you are interested in them, appreciate and value them, and respect their feelings. Nothing makes a person feel as accepted as really being listened to. Nothing makes a person feel as misunderstood and devalued as being ignored.

The fact is (and this is often overlooked by poor communicators): people are more interested in themselves and what they have to say than what you have to say. That's why popular people are nearly always attentive listeners. Think about it – don't you like it when someone gives you their undivided attention? That's why people are willing to pay good money for an hour with a therapist or life coach – to have someone really listen!

304

A good life coach spends about three-quarters of a session listening and one quarter talking. These are roughly the proportions you should aim to adopt when talking to others. When with others, talk less and listen more. When self-coaching, quieten your self-talk and listen carefully to your inner self.

305

Next time you talk to someone, note whether they really listen to you. Observe their facial expressions and body language carefully.

■ How do you know they're listening?

■ How do you know when someone switches off? What are the signs?

■ Do you ever do any of these?

306

Four levels of listening: good listening means becoming fully involved. The art of listening is not only to listen to the words but to the message behind the words. There are four main levels of listening:

1 Listening with little or no attention – your mind is elsewhere, absorbed in your own thoughts. You try to nod and mutter in the right place, but you're not really listening at all.

2 Informal listening – you only hear a small proportion of what is being said, because you're not giving it your full attention or are not particularly interested. This includes superficial interchanges at a bus

stop and casual conversations at social functions (i.e. 'small talk'). You just listen carefully enough to respond to polite questions such as 'how are you?' or remarks about the weather.

3 Perfect hearing – you're focused on the other person and giving them your full attention, as you do when attending a business briefing or a close friend is sharing their troubles with you. Perfect hearing can only happen if you are really interested and willing to stop what you're doing and concentrate. It goes beyond merely listening to words. You tune into the meaning conveyed through all the senses, including tone of voice, gestures and touch.

4 Intuitive listening – we sometimes get strong feelings about another person without necessarily knowing why – nothing that we're aware of in their speech or nonverbal signals explains it. For example, men are often puzzled by their wives' ability to sense what they are up to. As far as he knows he hasn't given her any tangible clues, yet somehow she knows. Ignore intuitive communication at your peril!

307

Consider:

■ How often do you pretend to listen – and don't really? Is there a pattern? When? With whom? Why?

■ How often do you listen with full attention? Is there a pattern? When? With whom? Why?

308

You'll need the help of a friend for this activity. Put aside 15 minutes. Decide who is to go first. This person talks for three minutes while the other listens. The listener must not say anything – no questions, interruptions, 'me-toos', etc. Just maintain gentle eye contact.

The listener now repeats back what they heard. How accurate is it?

Then reverse the roles. The second person talks for three minutes, the first listens, then checks that he or she heard correctly.

If you found this difficult, you are not a natural listener and need to practise this skill.

309

How good a listener are you? Most of us are poor listeners, and we communicate our lack of interest in many different ways. Here are a few (most of us are guilty of these from time to time). Which, if any, ever apply to you? Place a tick in the box, then think about what you can do to improve.

	Tick if applies to you	What can you do to improve?
Faking attention while thinking about something else.		
Showing impatience or irritation, e.g. playing with your fingers, doodling, humming, etc.		
Allowing yourself to be distracted by what's going on around you, e.g. watching TV or listening in on other conversations.		
Being put off by the other's appearance, accent or choice of words, etc.		
Being so preoccupied with getting your own ideas across you don't hear what others say.		
Impatience – unwillingness to devote time to listening.		
Switching off while you mentally rehearse your response.		
Trying to finish the sentence before the other has finished speaking.		
Switching off if you don't like what you hear.		

310

Words, voice and body language: only seven per cent of what you communicate comes across in the words used. For the remainder:

- Thirty-eight per cent is in *how* the words are spoken (quality of voice, tonality, voice projection, emphasis, expression, pace, volume, pitch, etc). For example, 'how do you mean?' can sound accusing, judgmental, considerate or humble depending on how the words are spoken.

- Body language (posture, position, eye contact, facial expression, head and body movements, gestures, touch, etc) accounts for 55 per cent.

Remember this when you speak – the *way* you talk reveals five times more than the words you use, and your *body* nearly eight times more. This is why we instinctively know when someone is lying. We pick up subtle signs from their voice and body language (e.g. untruths are often delivered in a higher pitch and with a shifty expression).

When words and non-verbals don't match, the latter are usually more reliable. For instance, if an agitated person attempts to hide anxiety by trying to sound relaxed, most people aren't fooled.

311

Reflect on this: What signals does *your* body send out as you speak? Are you happy with them? If not, how could you change them?

312

Stand in front of a mirror. If you have a tape or video recorder to hand, even better: record yourself as you do this exercise.

Repeat these words three times: 'So what was so wonderful about that?'

■ The first time, say them with a cruel sneer.

■ Then say them with sarcasm, ending with a sigh.

■ Finally, say them with genuine inquisitiveness, as if you really want to know the answer.

You'll notice that the meaning of this simple question can be completely ruined by the wrong tonality.

Eight rules of good listening

Which of these do you already do naturally? Which do you need to practise and improve?

313

Make time and be patient. This is the only way you can show respect and be fully present. Stop what you're doing and focus your full attention on listening and observing.

314

Take responsibility for making sure you understand their full meaning. If you don't hear first time, ask them to repeat it. If you don't understand, ask. If necessary, keep checking until you're sure you've understood.

315

Show that you are listening. Let them know they've been heard.
Memorise this useful mnemonic: **SOFTEN**:

Smile and project your warmth
Adopt an **O**pen posture (e.g. uncrossed arms/legs)
Lean towards them and **F**ace them squarely
Use **T**ouch (where appropriate)
Make **E**ye contact (but don't stare). Appropriate eye contact inspires
a feeling of trust and closeness.
Nod your head to signify understanding and/or approval.

Do these in a non-threatening manner. For example, touching another
person can be a gesture of support, but it can also be misinterpreted.
Similarly, while appropriate eye contact inspires a feeling of trust and
closeness, prolonged eye contact can be disconcerting. Hold your gaze
for long enough to acknowledge the other (three to four seconds is quite
sufficient), but not so long as to intimidate. A useful tip is to gaze at the
bridge of the nose rather than straight into the eyes – it's much less
intimidating.

316

Don't interrupt unless to ask a brief question to ensure you've really
understood. In the early days of telecommunication it was impossible to
speak and listen at the same time when talking on the telephone, and it's
no different today if both parties are listening well. If you catch yourself
interrupting, stop immediately, apologise, and invite them to continue.

Try this: when the speaker has finished talking, count to three and
wait before replying. This way you know they're not just stopping to
take a breath.

317

Learn to read body language. Listen with your ears *and* your eyes.

The human body is capable of transmitting over half a million signals, many of them subconsciously. The face alone can produce over a quarter of a million different expressions. A shrug of the shoulders, for instance, or a dismissive wave of the hand can express far more than words.

We are all continually telegraphing our thoughts, attitudes, feelings and intentions non-verbally. Here are some clues:

■ Eyes looking down or away – self-consciousness or guilt.

■ Raised eyebrow – disbelief.

■ Rubbing the nose or pulling the ears – they don't understand, even if they say they do.

■ Hand touching the mouth – anxious or trying to deceive you.

■ Folded or crossed arms – nervous or shut off from you (or feeling cold!).

■ Hands on hips or active gesturing – aggression.

■ Tapping on the desk or chair – nervousness or impatience.

■ Tremor in voice – nervousness.

■ Shrugging the shoulders – indifference to what you say.

■ Facing you squarely, full height, smiling, head forward – confidence.

Beware: body language is not universal – different cultures have their own gestures and ignorance can inadvertently result in offence.

318

Focus on the content. Ignore extraneous factors, such as appearance, dress sense, accent, choice of words, grammar, etc. Even if you find their language or ideas distasteful or offensive, keep listening. They won't open up to you if they think you're being prudish or condemning.

319

Check the accuracy of what you have heard. This reassures the other person that you have indeed been listening. There are two ways to do this:

First put what you've heard into your own words and subtly feed it back to the speaker. For example:

- 'You feel... because...' e.g. 'So you feel worried because you haven't heard from your mother for several weeks.'

- 'What I understand you to be saying is...'

- 'Let me make sure I understand you clearly...'

Alternatively, reflect back what you heard in different words:

- 'So you don't see much of a future in this job...'

- 'So you don't think the scheme will work...'

- 'It seems to me you don't think the relationship will last...'

If you're still not clear, ask directly for clarification.

- 'I'm sorry, I'm not sure I understand. Could you please explain...'

If this is a new skill for you, practise until you are confident you can do it without sounding like a mimic.

Secondly ask open-ended questions (see 108), such as:

- Tell me more about...

- How do you mean?

- In what way?

Open-ended questions keep the other person talking and encourage them to explain themselves fully.

320

Learn to cope with silence; most people find silence uncomfortable.
Good listeners resist the tendency to jump in when the other person
stops talking. During periods of silence the speaker's mind is still active
and often moments of profound insight take place. Shut up and be
patient, no matter how disconcerting it feels.

Representational systems

Most life coaches are skilled in the use of Neuro-Linguistic Programming (NLP), a set
of techniques developed by Richard Bandler and John Grinder in the 1970s. NLP is a
collection of highly effective concepts, tools and procedures based on a profound
understanding of the mind. You can use NLP techniques to enhance your listening
abilities, build rapport with anyone, and improve your understanding of yourself and
others.

321

Our brains process and store our experiences in terms of our five senses.
We perceive ourselves, others, our environment and what is going on
around us and store it in terms of these five sensory systems:

- Seeing (visual).

- Hearing (auditory).

- Feeling (kinesthetic).

- Smelling (olfactory).

- Tasting (gustatory).

Every experience you have had may be recalled in any one, or a
combination, of these **representational systems**.

Say you once attended a wedding. If you put your mind to it you can
probably remember the interior of the church, the bride's dress, the
vicar's voice, exchange of rings, the sound and resonance of the music,
the hardness of the pews and so on. A thousand other details may be
recalled in a combination of sights, smells, sounds, tastes, moods and
textures.

Although nearly everyone can access all five sensory systems, we all tend to have our favourites. Some feel more natural, more comfortable:

■ Auditory people respond most readily to sound/what they hear.

■ Visual people tend to think in pictures.

■ Kinesthetic people prefer to rely on their sense of touch.

Gustatory (taste) and olfactory (smell) are the minor senses.

When two people who share the same primary representational systems converse, there is usually instant rapport. Conversely, a visual person, say, in conversation with an auditory or kinesthetic may have difficulty establishing rapport.

You will communicate most effectively if you tailor your speech to the other person's preferred representational system. Similarly, you will feel more 'tuned in' to someone who shares, or is able to adapt, to yours.

How can you spot the preferred representational system of another, especially if you're meeting them for the first time?

There are several ways, but these are the best:

■ Listen carefully to the speaker's language (this is the 'linguistic' part of Neuro-Linguistic Programming).

■ Ask smart questions.

322

Close your eyes. Think of a pleasant experience. Picture it in your mind – what can you see? Recall the sounds – what can you hear? How did it feel – what are you feeling now? What smells and tastes does it elicit?

Which sense is the easiest to recreate? Most difficult? Impossible?

This exercise will help you to identify your preferred representational system(s).

323

Linguistic giveaways. People reveal their preferred representation system in the words they use. Listen carefully. If you are perceptive, you will detect certain patterns of speech.

For example:

Visual	Auditory
'I see what you mean.' 'The way I look at it is...' 'Let me put you in the picture.' 'It's not as black and white as it seems.' 'We don't see eye to eye.' 'It's crystal clear.' 'There's a light at the end of the tunnel.' 'Show me what you mean.'	'I hear what you say.' 'I like the sound of this.' 'We're speaking the same language.' 'I'm lost for words.' 'It doesn't strike a chord with me.' 'It doesn't ring any bells.' 'Tell me what you mean.'
Kinesthetic	**Gustatory**
'He rubs me up the wrong way.' 'I can't get a handle on that.' 'It doesn't feel right to me.' 'We're going through a rough patch.' 'He's a cool customer.' 'I feel it in my bones.' 'It sends a shiver down my spine.' 'Give yourself a pat on the back.'	'It leaves a bitter/sour taste in the mouth.' 'I no longer have the appetite for it.' 'He bit off more than he could chew.' 'She tasted success at an early age.' **Olfactory** 'I don't like the smell of that.' 'Something fishy's going on.' 'It stinks!'

Some words are not sensory based, including many which we associate with abstract ideas and the intuition – think, know, understand, recognise, remember, learn, interpret, etc.

Once you're tuned in to the other person you can adapt your language to their representational system and will find that the conversation flows better.

Pick three people you know well. Next time you meet, listen carefully. Identify their preferred representational system. Try to amend your language to accommodate their style. What effect does this have on your interaction?

324

A second useful way to identify another's preferred representational system is to ask them to describe something or say how they feel about it. For example, 'Tell me about your home. What do you like best about where you live?' Then prompt. 'What else?' 'What don't you like?' 'How do you feel about that?'

The reply could be most illuminating. 'The peace and quiet.' 'The garden is absolutely beautiful in summer.' 'The décor.' 'It's warm and comfortable.' 'It doesn't get the sun.' 'It's overlooked by the neighbours,' etc. Everything they say offers more clues.

Metaphors

325

Noticing and understanding **metaphors**. A metaphor is a story, illustration or figure of speech which likens one thing (such as an idea or concept) to another. The two things may bear little resemblance to each other, but enable us to gain a better understanding. For instance, there's no such thing as an 'icy glance' or 'nerves of steel', and no one really speaks with a plum in their mouth, but we know what they mean.

When we likened the goal-seeking mechanism within the subconscious to a nuclear missile seeking out its target, we were using a metaphor.

Listen carefully for metaphors. They reveal a great deal about a person's attitudes, values and view of the world.

For example:

'Life is a bowl of cherries.'

'Life's a bitch and then you die.'

'I was born under a lucky star.'

'Life is a journey.'

'Life isn't a bed of roses.'

'Trying to get any sense out of him is like pulling teeth.'

'Every cloud has a silver lining.'

Metaphors are often used unconsciously. Sometimes the speaker inadvertently reveals something about themselves. That's why they are such a valuable source of insight and information for the perceptive and willing listener.

326

Listen to your self-talk and monitor yourself in conversation.

- What metaphors do you use frequently?

- What do they say about you as a person – your way of looking at the world, your attitudes, beliefs, etc?

Rapport

Rapport is an agreeable relationship in which there is a common understanding and usually an emotional bond or connection between the individuals concerned. Rapport creates a climate of trust which makes an interaction smoother. You don't have to like someone to be in rapport with them (but it helps).

327

The essence of building rapport quickly is to act on the old proverbs 'like attracts like' and 'birds of a feather stick together.' In other words, look for as much as possible that you have in common.

- Agree with the other person as much as possible, and let as much go as you can. This doesn't mean pretending to be something you're not, just making it easier for them to get along with you.

- Relate similar interests and experiences. Talk about places visited, mutual friends, concerts, exhibitions or sporting events. Seek out shared hobbies and pastimes, but don't go in for one-upmanship and don't pretend to know anything you don't.

- However, steer clear of lies and empty promises. There's no point in pretending you love playing golf and offering to give them a game sometime if you hate golf and don't know an 'eagle' from any other sort of 'birdie'. They might challenge you to a game!

Some people are naturally good at establishing rapport and others have to learn, but it is a skill everyone can acquire.

328

Establishing rapport: matching and mirroring. A mirror reflects what is in front of it. The NLP technique of mirroring – which is a means of establishing rapid rapport – does the same.

Watch any couple who are getting on well. What do you see? If one leans forward and smiles, so does the other. If one talks in a hushed tone, the other does too. She crosses her legs and folds her arms, so does he. He smiles and shakes his head and, guess what? She does too. The couples aren't deliberately mimicking each other. It's just that when people are getting on well with someone else they subconsciously adopt similar non-verbals.

Emulating another's body language and speech patterns is a sure-fire way to deepen your rapport. Subtly adapt your breathing patterns, pace of speech, tone of voice, posture, body language and facial expression to the other person's. Borrow their words and expressions. This must of course be done skillfully, or they'll think you are ridiculing them. The last thing you want is to come across as a parrot, but with practise you'll be able to do it without any hint of mimicry.

After mirroring them by gradually changing your speech and breathing patterns, you will find they begin to follow you. In NLP this is called **matching** and is frequently taught to salespeople.

329

Mismatching. The techniques for building rapport also work in reverse. If you want to end a conversation, deliberately mismatch.

■ Turn away.

■ Adjust your body language so that it is different to theirs.

■ Pick up a pen and start writing.

■ Look at your watch.

■ Use auditory words if they are not an auditory person, visual words if they are not a visual person and kinesthetic words if they are not a kinesthetic person.

■ Speak quickly to a slow talker, or vice-versa.

They soon get the message!

Conversational skills

330

A skilled communicator can put almost anyone at ease. This is your aim too – to make them feel good and relieve any discomfort, especially if they are shy.

Good conversational skills are not only a terrific advantage in your personal life, they are also a great asset in the world of business. Top business executives know that 'small talk leads to big talk'. Many a profitable deal which proved impossible to negotiate in a conventional business setting has been struck over a restaurant table or on a golf course.

Do you regard 'small talk' as a waste of time? If so, you'll never be any good at it and, what's more, people sense your irritation and avoid you. Practise making small talk until you're accomplished at it. Good listeners who are genuinely interested in others never find it a chore.

Initiating a conversation

331

First impressions last: the first few seconds of any conversation set the tone, starting from the moment you notice each other. First impressions remain in the memory a long time and may be recalled every time they think of you, so it's vital to get off on the right footing. Be polite, genuine and sincere from the outset; show that you respect the other person.

Do your homework. If possible find out about people you're going to meet beforehand, their work, leisure activities, family background, etc. If you've met them before, cast your mind back. Where was it? What did you talk about? What did you learn about their interests and outlook on life?

If you're entering a business environment, prepare yourself. Think carefully about what you want from the conversation, what you are going to say and how you intend to say it. If you think this sounds cold and calculating, bear in mind that a professional sales person, interviewer or negotiator will have done their homework on you.

332

Act confidently. If others detect nervousness in you they feel uneasy. Apply the 'as if' principle. Put a smile on your face (this is probably the most important thing you can do, especially if you're shy), ignore the collywobbles in your stomach and act the part of a self-assured, cheerful, enthusiastic person.

Work on developing a steady gaze. When with a group, move your gaze round steadily; if you restrict your gaze to one or two people, the others feel excluded. If speaking to a shy person, look but don't stare.

Make as much eye contact when you speak as when you listen. Look steadily and gently, then look away. Let them know it's safe and comfortable for them to make eye contact with you.

333

To appear confident even if you're not:

■ Stand tall. The bigger you appear, the more authoritative.

■ Offer your hand first, state your name and look inquiringly so they volunteer theirs.

■ Keep your hands still and away from your face.

■ Make your head movements smooth and don't tilt it sideways (unless you want to look cute!).

■ Keep your head up to avoid looking submissive – but not too high: looking down your nose appears arrogant.

■ Avoid jerky movements and unnecessary gesticulations.

334

Getting to know each other. Give the other person a 'verbal handle' to grab hold of, that gets them talking about themselves and their interests.

Note: *their* interests, not yours!

Ask open-ended questions to keep the momentum going, but avoid questions which are controversial or potentially embarrassing. Talk about current news stories by all means, but avoid subjects such as politics until you know them better, otherwise you might find the conversation coming to an abrupt halt.

If you know anything about them, use what you know. Ask about their family, home, hobbies, work, holidays, travel, sporting interests, musical and literary preferences, or whatever seems appropriate. If possible, choose topics in which you're well versed.

■ How's your family, Harry? Has your wife recovered from her illness?

■ I've heard you paint in your spare time. Tell me more about your work.

■ How's the golf going these days, Alan?

■ Is it true you live on a house boat, Jennifer? Sounds fascinating – tell me about it.

■ How's your daughter settling in at university, Steve?

■ Heard any more about that job you applied for, Claire?'

Be sensitive, of course. This isn't an interrogation.

335

Appeal to their need for approval. We are all motivated to some extent by a need for approval. Praise, appreciation and gratitude are always well received, providing it doesn't come over as insincere (which means words, voice and non-verbals must be congruent). Use 'please' and 'thank you' whenever appropriate and warmly comment on the things you appreciate about others.

336

Lighten up. Observe yourself in conversation. Do you:

- Say 'I' often?

- Complain frequently?

- Over-analyse?

- Talk frequently about your problems?

- Readily dismiss new ideas?

- Fail to see the funny side?

If you answered 'yes' to any of these questions, you need to lighten up. Nobody likes talking to someone who is self-centred, closed, or over serious.

337

Establish a reputation for honesty, reliability and integrity. Never make promises you don't intend to honour. Be sincere and always keep your word.

If you gain a reputation for not meaning what you say and letting people down, people will become wary of you. It could take a long time to repair the damage.

338

Stop talking before your audience stops listening. You don't want to be remembered as a bit of a bore. If it is clear they have heard enough and want to move on, politely bring the conversation to a close (use 'mismatching' if apt). Don't be like the woman about whom George Bernard Shaw wrote, 'She had lost the art of conversation but not, unfortunately, the power of speech!'

339

Experiment. Use the above techniques in your conversations for a week. Keep a log of your experiences in your Self-Coaching Journal. What has changed in the way others respond to you?

Evaluate the results, make some adjustments if necessary, then do the same for another week. Keep going until it feels natural.

12 ASSERTIVENESS

> *This above all: to thine own self be true*
> *And it must follow, as the night the day,*
> *Thou canst not then be false to any man.*
>
> **William Shakespeare**

Imagine this scene. It's a cold Wednesday evening in December and getting late – 10.30 p.m. The telephone rings. The caller, a young woman, informs you that she's phoning to confirm the delivery tomorrow morning of the kitchen cabinets you ordered. You're puzzled. You distinctly recall telling the salesman that you wanted them delivered on Friday, and watched as he made a note of it on the order form. You point this out to the young woman.

'But it's in the schedule,' she insists. 'It's already arranged. It's on the computer.'

What would you do?

This actually happened to a client, Ray, recently. Ray is a retired businessman who was planning a day out with his wife the following day as a pre-Christmas treat. He could have backed down, cancelled his other plans and agreed to the delivery (as scores of people would). He could have grown angry and snapped at the caller (again, many would). He did neither. He simply repeated what he'd already said. He knew she was probably following instructions, but still, he wanted the delivery date changed, so he calmly told her that it was not convenient.

She protested. 'The lorry was loaded earlier this evening; it's too late to change it now.'

'I'm sorry,' said Ray, 'I've told you it's not convenient.'

'But there's nothing I can do now. We'll have to deliver tomorrow.' Her voice was trembling. Ray wondered if she was going to be in trouble with her boss, but that was not his concern.

'Once again, please listen,' he said calmly. 'I've told you it's not convenient. Now please do whatever you have to do to make alternative arrangements and let me know the result.' Then he wished her good night and replaced the receiver.

Ray's reply was the perfect assertive response. Assertiveness is stating your point of view honestly and firmly, while respecting the other person's right to hold a different opinion. You express yourself clearly, honouring your own needs and values while at the same time respecting the dignity of others.

Assertiveness is an essential skill for several reasons:

- It enables you to deal more effectively with difficult situations.

- It prevents your being steamrollered into agreeing to something against your better judgement.

- It's good for your physical and emotional wellbeing, because (once you've got used to being assertive) it lowers your stress levels.

- It promotes understanding. Everyone concerned understands each other better. Without it, no one is being totally honest.

Assertiveness is closely tied to your confidence and self-esteem. People with low self-esteem often find it difficult to be honest with themselves and open with other people.

Assertiveness is often misunderstood. Some think it means being loud and pushy and acting selfishly. This is far from the truth. When you value yourself, you value others more too. Crucial to genuine assertiveness is empathy – understanding and respecting the other person's point of view.

340

How assertive are you? Do you find it difficult to be honest with yourself? Are you open and truthful with other people? If not, why do you think this is?

How likely is it that it has something to do with your self-esteem?

341

Make a list of occasions in the past when you did not say what you meant or neglected to stand up for yourself.

Now make a list of specific situations in which you would like to be more assertive in the future, or people with whom you would like to be more assertive, e.g. at work, in shops and restaurants, with your boss, pushy salespeople, your spouse, parents, or children, etc.

342

Assertive behaviour is:

- Saying what you think and how you feel calmly and politely.

- Making your point clearly and with conviction.

- Being in touch with your intuition and inner desires, and trusting and valuing them.

- Expressing your feelings honestly and with consideration for others.

- Sticking to your point. If necessary, repeating it until you've achieved your preferred outcome.

- Standing up for your rights without violating the rights of others.

- Being clear on what you want and asking for it.

- Knowing when to 'chill out' and when to 'come on strong'.

- Never deliberately hurting others' feelings.

If you haven't been assertive until now, this is the time to start. You may feel uncomfortable to start with, but don't be put off. Practise! The rewards are too great to ignore.

343

Do you believe you always have the right to:

	Yes?	No?
Express your feelings		
Stand up for your opinions		
Make requests		
Refuse requests		
Change your mind without offering an explanation		
Say 'I don't know' or 'I don't understand'		
Refuse to justify your behaviour		

If you have answered 'no' to any of these questions, why do you think that is? All these are fundamental human rights, so make a commitment to change.

Eight ways to become more assertive

The keys to being assertive are:

■ Effective listening.

■ Showing the other person that you fully understand, or are eager to understand, what they are saying.

■ Willingness to compromise and adopt joint solutions, i.e. being prepared to give and take. Assertive people recognise that others have legitimate rights and needs, and try to accommodate them in ways which are acceptable to both.

■ Integrity; keeping your word. Broken promises always return to haunt you.

Even if you've never considered yourself particularly assertive, mastering a few basic skills can bring rapid progress.

344

Listen carefully. Become a good listener. Show the other person that you are interested and understand what they are saying. Otherwise you may be responding to something you haven't heard and the other person didn't mean.

345

Do it now. Timing is important. If you are upset by someone's words or actions, challenge them now. Don't wait – the opportunity may not come and you may find yourself churning over what you wish you'd said.

It's always better (and less stressful) to tackle a situation as it occurs than say or do nothing and allow it to get worse.

346

Adopt assertive body language and tone of voice:

- Adopt an assertive tone of voice. Speak and breathe unhurriedly – assertive people talk with a steady, clear tone and breathe slowly as they speak. Take your time. If you speak too fast or gabble, your words lack authority.

- Eye contact and gestures are important. Shifty, wandering eyes denote lack of confidence or lack of trustworthiness; conversely, a hard stare is intimidating. Give relaxed eye contact – not too little, not too much.

- Take in a breath before you're ready to speak. This helps you to be more self-composed.

- Hands are very expressive. Impatient, forceful gestures are threatening. Fidgeting, scratching and constantly touching your hair and face indicate tension.

- Develop a firm handshake – it denotes strength and integrity.

- Use silence to your advantage. Silence can be intimidating. It can indicate that you're too upset or frightened to speak, or have nothing to say. It can also be empowering.

- Use personal space. The more space you take up, the more important you appear. On the other hand, moving too close is unsettling. So get close – but not too close!

- Posture is important. An upright stance makes you look more important, even if you're not especially tall. It makes you look younger and slimmer too. Carry yourself as if you are worth taking notice of. Stand tall, neck and shoulders relaxed, arms loose at your side. Sit up straight, and avoid crossing your legs and folding your arms – this indicates a defensive attitude

---

347

Be specific: don't beat about the bush. Make your point clearly and with conviction. Say it calmly but firmly. Never say anything you don't really mean.

If you find this difficult, you may have to confront your fears. Why are you afraid to speak your mind? What's the worst that could happen? Is it anything more than the other person disagreeing with you or refusing to go along with your ideas? If so – that's not really scary at all, is it?

348

Refer to the *behaviour* you find upsetting and say how it affects you. Attacking a person's character or integrity is an act of aggression and usually self-defeating. It gets their back up and makes it unlikely they will want listen to you. So if you feel you have to criticise, always restrict your remarks to their behaviour rather than having a go at the individual. Express your feelings openly.

Tell them how you feel about it – you have a perfect right to do so. If you wish, you may diffuse tension by being open. 'I feel awkward about saying (or asking you) this, but I'd like you to...'

349

Say what you would like to happen next. Keep in mind what you would like to happen as a result of your words. For example, if someone is gossiping about your friend, say to them: 'I don't like it when you talk about my friend like that. It doesn't reflect well on you and makes me feel very unhappy. I would like you to promise to stop it, please.'

Here's a form of words you can use when you want to ask someone to change their behaviour:

'When you... I feel uncomfortable/it makes me feel... and if it continues/if you don't stop... I want you to...'

350

Use silence to your advantage. Silence can be uncomfortable. It can indicate that a person is upset or too frightened to speak, or have nothing to say.

But it can also be empowering. If you can handle silence better than others, you're in the driving seat. Make your point, then stay quiet. Stay calm and relaxed while the other person considers their response. Observe carefully.

351

Persevere. If you are being ignored or not taken seriously, simply repeat the essential parts of your message and, if necessary, keep repeating it. Change the words used if you wish, but not the message. Avoid being sidetracked.

Obviously you won't always get your own way, but if you say it right at least you've made your mark, you'll feel better about yourself and you will almost certainly be taken more seriously in future. And if you find you have to go along with actions you didn't support and it doesn't work out, you can point out that didn't do it willingly.

352

A few words of warning. Your friends and colleagues may have problems adjusting to the new self-confident and assertive you. They may even feel threatened by it.

Don't be put off. You won't want to be knocked back to where you were, and why should you? Just be sensitive to their feelings until they've got used to the new you.

353

Asking for what you want. You'd be amazed how many opportunities open up to you when you know how to ask for what you want.

■ Be clear on the outcome you want.

■ Choose the right time and place.

■ Ask the right person – someone who is potentially willing and able to grant your request – and make sure you have their full attention.

■ Work out what you're going to say beforehand.

■ Be specific. If you need help, what kind of help? From whom?

■ Don't apologise. Avoid phrases like: 'I'm afraid' and 'I'm sorry but…'

■ Think of the benefits to the other person and, if it helps your case, point them out.

■ Don't be sidetracked. If the other person won't agree, keep repeating your request.

■ Anticipate their reaction and work out a strategy in advance. Mentally rehearse your response.

■ If your request is rejected or ignored, calmly and persistently repeat your demand as many times as necessary.
  • 'You may not have heard me but…'
  • 'Let me say it again…'
  • 'But the point is…'

- Ask for the reason for their refusal. Bear in mind that the explanation given at first may not be the real reason, so keep asking 'Why?' 'Why not?'
- If this still doesn't work try showing that you understand the other person's point of view before repeating the request. 'I realise that… but I still want you to…'

■ If you still don't get what you want, learn from your experience and apply it next time.

■ Accept the outcome politely and with gratitude.

---

354 How to say 'no' (and make it sound like a compliment). Many people find saying 'no' problematical. They want to be liked, but in the long run only create a far worse situation by saying 'yes' when they don't mean it. The secret is to find a pleasant way to say 'no', stay calm and hold firm.

■ Smile, use a pleasant tone of voice and warm, open body language to show the other person you aren't being unkind.

■ Make it clear that you are rejecting the request, not the person.

■ It's often a good idea to soften your answer so as not to offend. For instance:
  - 'I'd prefer not to…'
  - 'That's a wonderful offer, but I'm not interested at present.'
  - 'I'm sorry you've got that problem, but there's nothing I can do.'
  - 'I'd love to help, but it's just not possible.'
  - 'It's a good idea, but I can't work on it with you at the moment.'

■ Use humour if appropriate.

■ Show that you've understood the request, and make the reply short and to the point, e.g. 'I realise that… (paraphrase their proposition) but the answer is no.'

■ Try complimenting the other person before refusing, e.g. 'I admire your charity and the work you do, but I don't wish to place an advertisement in your magazine at this time.'

■ If they persist, hold firm. Only change your mind if you want to. A useful tactic is to say, 'You aren't trying to pressure me, are you?' Nine times out of ten they'll back down.

■ Don't apologise nor feel obliged to justify your decision.

■ Stall if necessary. You can always ask for more time to think it over if you are undecided. Say 'Let me think about that before I answer.' This allows you to become aware of what you really want or don't want.

■ Silence can be very effective, e.g. 'I'm sorry you've got that problem.' Then stop talking and wait for a response. You don't have to play 'rescuer'.

At times, there's no way round it – you just have to say 'no' and keep saying 'no' until they get the message.

13 Happiness – the point of it all

> " *Happiness consists more in small conveniences or pleasures that occur every day, than in great pieces of good fortune that happen but seldom to a man in the course of his life.*
>
> **Benjamin Franklin** "

What part does happiness play in your hopes? You'd be a very unusual person if it didn't feature somewhere. After all, we're born into the world without really knowing why we're here and die generally none the wiser – surely we want to enjoy as much as possible of the time in between.

Can happiness be taught? Some psychologists think not – they tell us that some are just born 'the happy type'. But many believe that happiness can be taught. I've seen it for myself. A friend of mine, Alan Davidson, has been teaching happiness for many years around the South of England and the results are dramatic. His students frequently report that their whole lives have been turned around.

Can we set happiness as a goal just like any other and work towards it, just as we would work towards any other goal? Or can we become happy simply by changing our way of thinking? Let's examine these in detail.

355

How happy are you? Write down a number between zero and ten, where ten signifies that you are blissfully happy all the time, and zero that you are totally, irretrievably and permanently miserable.

How happy would you like to be on a scale of zero to ten? (If you score yourself less than ten, why is this?)

356

Studies show that happy people tend to:

■ Be hopeful about the future.

■ Enjoy good health.

■ Have a wide range of rewarding pastimes and hobbies.

■ Avoid indulging in blame and self-pity.

■ Make the most of things as they are.

■ Enjoy warm family relationships.

■ See the funny side of life.

■ Have work that is enjoyable and fulfilling.

■ Be people-orientated.

■ Refuse to dwell on their troubles.

■ Use their time productively.

■ Have close friends of both genders.

Which of these apply to you?

If *all* applied, would you be happier? Then add them to your list of goals or qualities you wish to acquire (if you haven't already). Each and every one can be learned and developed using the ITIA formula and TGROW approach.

357

Are you relying on achieving your goals to make you happy? If so, beware.

Studies show that people who believe that achieving their goals will make them happy are usually disappointed. They easily become frustrated by the gap between their aspirations and their actual achievements, and are prone to stress-related illness. You will never be truly happy if your happiness depends on your achievements. Why? Because:

1   The idea that happiness will automatically be bestowed on you when some future event takes place is a fallacy, unless you are reasonably happy to start with and approach your activities with eagerness and joy.

2   Goals anticipate and look to the future, but happiness can only exist in the here and now.

3   Happiness is an inner state. You can't buy or sell it, wear it or drive it, go on holiday to it or receive it as a gift. Some live in poverty and are happy; others are worth millions, but are not. This is probably not what you've been taught – plenty of people have a vested interest in persuading you that only by buying their products can you find contentment.

Moreover, if your happiness depends on what others think of you, you're giving them the power to choose your emotional state. You can't control the thoughts, feelings, words or actions of others, and it's a fact of life that you won't get on with everyone and not everyone you meet will like you.

So is there any truth in the idea that happiness is a choice you make by adopting a certain way of thinking. Was Abraham Lincoln right when he said, 'Most folks are about as happy as they make up their minds to be'?

Yes – to some extent, but it isn't the whole story. Happiness is a combination of *attitude* and *emotion*, and as we know, permanent and lasting change only comes about when *all four* elements of the ITIA formula – intention + thought + imagination + action – are applied.

Seven keys to happiness

358

Self-acceptance is a prerequisite of genuine happiness. It is impossible to be happy unless you are first able to love and acknowledge yourself as you are, warts'n'all. If you believe that you will only be able to accept yourself after you've achieved all your goals, you're mistaken. Self-acceptance is a necessary step in the process; it leads to success, not the other way round. There's nothing wrong with wanting to achieve, but needing to achieve brings nothing but unhappiness. Many who are driven to achieve don't find happiness even when they succeed.

No amount of knowledge, skills, accolades and accomplishments can compensate for a lack of self-acceptance. (If you need help, I recommend my book *365 Steps to Self-Confidence* – see Appendix.)

359

Are you *willing* to be happy? Write down your answers to the following questions;

- What *absolutely must* happen or be present for me to be happy?

- What would I *prefer* to happen or be present for me to be happy?

Your answers indicate your 'rules' for happiness. These are your beliefs about the conditions that have to be met for you to feel happy. Over-zealous rules can literally wipe out your chances of ever being happy.

Let's take an example. An elderly friend of mine, a lady of modest means, suffers from Parkinson's disease, and is one of the happiest people I know. 'Every morning when I wake up' she says, 'I look out of the window. The sun is shining, the birds are singing and I tell myself it's another wonderful day. I have a loving family, lots of friends and I'm glad to be alive.'

When asked about her condition, she says, 'It's inconvenient, but it doesn't hurt, and thanks to the medication, I can live virtually a normal life.' Her 'rules for happiness' are so simple, it's almost impossible for her to be sad.

How about you? Are you willing to be happy? Then examine your rules for happiness. If they're too complicated, rigid or numerous, simplify them. Then resolve to live by your new rules.

360

Realise that happiness is much more than fun. Fun is important. I urge you to have as much fun as you can, so long as you don't equate happiness with fun alone. Happy people certainly have fun, but they're not the same.

Fun activities bring pleasure, make us laugh and temporarily forget our problems, but the effect soon diminishes once the activity ends. If you seek endless fun you'll have an empty, longing feeling once the party is over, because you're not addressing some of the other important issues that bring *genuine* happiness.

True happiness demands accepting the highs and lows, the rough and the smooth, the ups and downs of life. Happiness is *not* merely an absence of problems. Life is a school – look for the lessons in every situation, and welcome problems as challenges to be turned into opportunities using your ingenuity.

361

Mix with happy people. Happiness is infectious. It rubs off. So does unhappiness.

Get caught up in the happiness spiral. Work on your own happiness so you can spread it to others and attract happy people who infect you with their zest for life. Mix with people who know how to enjoy themselves, but also have a sense of purpose and enthusiasm. Life is meant to be exciting and enjoyable.

362

Laugh loud and laugh often. The ability to laugh is one of the best indications of good physical and mental health. We feel good when we laugh; it alters our body chemistry, flooding the bloodstream with the happy hormones, endorphins, which bring about powerful feel-good sensations.

When we feel good we laugh and smile. It also works in reverse. When we laugh and smile we feel good. Read funny books, watch funny TV programmes, films and DVDs, and mix with people who share your sense of humour. And practise the 'inner smile': the more you smile inwardly to yourself, the more you'll experience a sense of happiness and wellbeing.

363

Count your blessings. Keep your thoughts on all the good things in your life, including those you love and love you. List them in your Self-Coaching Journal. Read them through often. Add to them whenever you can.

All happy people have an attitude of gratitude. Count your blessings every day.

364

Be here now. One of the biggest steps you can take to happiness and peace of mind is learning to appreciate the 'here and now'.

At this moment you are reading this sentence. You may also have one eye on the TV and be vaguely aware of other people around you. You may be lying on a beach or out in the countryside. At this precise moment all is well in your world.

Whatever happened in the past – last year, last week, five minutes ago – is gone forever. You can't change it. Learn from your yesterdays, but don't cling to them. And who knows how many more precious moments like these await you tomorrow, the day after, next week…

How can you ever be happy if you constantly agonise over past mistakes and wish you could go back and relive parts of your past? Change your self-talk; visualise something different, and stop complaining, blaming and criticising yourself.

You can only live one day at a time. Now is the only moment over which you have control, so make the most of it. And remember the last line of *Gone With The Wind* – 'Tomorrow is another day!'

Dr Usui's Five Principles

1   Just for today, I am choosing not to feel anger about things I used to feel angry about.

2   Just for today, I am choosing not to worry about things I used to worry about.

3   Just for today, I am going to find satisfaction or enjoyment in more and more of what I do.

4   Just for today, I am going to work on my own wellbeing and health, learning the skills to allow me to take control.

5   Just for today, I am going to be kind to others (even if I have to do it through gritted teeth initially!).

(Dr Usui was the reviver of Reiki healing and the founder of the modern system of healing that bears his name.)

365

The final secret of happiness is to understand that it is not the achievement of our goals that brings happiness, but the sense of purpose and direction they bring. Ironically, whether you actually achieve them is almost immaterial. Providing you are not selfishly motivated, the attempt alone provides the sense of satisfaction you seek. The primary reward, to quote author David McNally, 'is not the goal, but what you become as a result of doing all that was necessary to reach the goal.'

If you succeed – great! If not, at least you've enjoyed trying. But you probably will. When you find what you love, put your heart and soul into it and make sure it benefits others as well as yourself, your life takes on new meaning and everything works out entirely for the best.

"

Forget about you and all the things you're going to get out of what you're doing. Simply go out, head in the direction of your dreams, live your own kind of life, and success will chase after you and arrive in amounts greater than anticipated.

Dr Wayne Dyer "

Appendix

Photocopy this page.

Where do you intend to be six months from now?

a) Write down at least three goals that you would like to have achieved six months from now.
1
2
3
b) Write down what you intend to do to achieve each of these goals.
Goal 1:
Goal 2:
Goal 3:
Your name and address:

Now send a copy of this to me at 14 Stanfield Road, Bournemouth BH9 2NW, United Kingdom, together with a stamped addressed envelope. I'll post it back to you six months after I receive it. I guarantee you'll be amazed at how much progress you've made!

References and further reading

Dale Carnegie, *How to Win Friends and Influence People*, Vermilion, London, 1990.

Lewis Carroll, *Alice in Wonderland*, Penguin, London, 1994.

Stephen Covey, *The Seven Habits of Highly Effective People,* Simon and Schuster, London, 1992.

Arianna Huffington, *The Fourth Instinct*, Simon and Schuster, New York, 2003.

Vera Peiffer, *Positive Thinking*, Harper Collins, London, 2001.

Tony Buzan, *How to Mind Map: The Ultimate Thinking Tool That Will Change Your Life*, Harper Collins, London, 2002.

Richard Bandler and John Grinder, *The Structure of Magic*, Science and Behavior Books, Palo Alto CA, 1989.

Suggested reading

There are many books available with the words 'life coach' in the title. In my opinion, these are the best of them:

Eileen Mulligan, *Life Coaching: Change your life in 7 days,* Piatkus, London, 1999.

Curly Martin, *The Life Coaching Handbook,* Crown House, Carmarthen, 2001.

Julie Starr, *The Coaching Manual,* Pearson Education Ltd, Edinburgh, 2003.

Other books worth consulting are:

Richard Bandler and John Grinder, *Frogs Into Princes*, Real People Press, Moab, 1979.

Dr Wayne Dyer, *Your Erroneous Zones,* Time Warner Paperbacks, New York, 1992.

Dr Wayne Dyer, *Manifest Your Destiny,* Thorson Element Books, London, 2003.

Dr Viktor E. Frankl, *Man's Search for Meaning,* Pocket Books, New York, 1984.

Dr Napolean Hill, *Think and Grow Rich,* Ballantine Publishing, New York, 1996.

Dr Susan Jeffers, *Feel the Fear and Do It Anyway,* Arrow Books Ltd, London, 1987.

Byron Katie, *Loving What Is,* Rider & Co, London, 2002.

Amanda Lowe, *Bliss,* Crown House, Carmarthen, 2004.

David Lawrence Preston, *365 Steps to Self-Confidence*, How To Books, 2001.

Anthony Robbins, *Unlimited Power,* Simon and Schuster, London, 1988.

David Swindley, *Only the Truth Shall Set You Free,* Inner Power Publications, Bournemouth, 1998.

Michael Tipper, *The Secrets of Successful Students,* Lucky Duck Publishing, Bristol, 2002.

Nick Williams, *The Work We Were Born to Do,* Element Books, Shaftesbury, 1999.

Paramahansa Yogananda, *To Be Victorious In Life,* Self Realization Fellowship, Los Angeles, 2002.

Newcastle College offers an excellent fully accredited distance learning Certificate and Diploma in Life Coaching. These are free of charge to UK citizens. For further details write to Newcastle College Flexible Learning, Manor Walks, Cramlington NE23 6QW.

Index

Name index

Subject Index